# CAN I GET A WITNESS?

**Also by Julia A. Boyd**

*In the Company of My Sisters*
*Girlfriend to Girlfriend*
*Embracing the Fire*

# CAN I GET A WITNESS?

*For Sisters When the*
*Blues Is More Than a Song*

## JULIA A. BOYD

A DUTTON BOOK

DUTTON
Published by the Penguin Group
Penguin Putnam Inc., 375 Hudson Street,
New York, New York 10014, U.S.A.
Penguin Books Ltd, 27 Wrights Lane,
London W8 5TZ, England
Penguin Books Australia Ltd, Ringwood,
Victoria, Australia
Penguin Books Canada Ltd, 10 Alcorn Avenue,
Toronto, Ontario, Canada M4V 3B2
Penguin Books (N.Z.) Ltd, 182–190 Wairau Road,
Auckland 10, New Zealand

Penguin Books Ltd, Registered Offices:
Harmondsworth, Middlesex, England

First published by Dutton, an imprint of Dutton NAL,
a member of Penguin Putnam Inc.

First Printing, September, 1998
10   9   8   7   6   5   4   3   2   1

LIBRARY OF CONGRESS CATALOGING-IN-PUBLICATION DATA:

Boyd, Julia A.
    Can I get a witness? : for sisters when the blues is more than a song / Julia A. Boyd.
        p.   cm.
    Includes bibliographical references.
    ISBN 0-525-94446-X (acid-free paper)
    1. Afro-American women—Psychology.   2. Afro-American women—Life skills guides.   3. Depression, Mental.   I. Title.
    E185.86.B645   1998
    305.48'896073—dc21                                        98-24279
                                                               CIP

Printed in the United States of America
Set in Candida
Designed by Leonard Telesca

To Momi
Lavada Conyers (1924–1994)

To Daddy
Joseph Conyers (1925– )

With all my love

# Acknowledgments

I thank God every day for blessing me with all the wonderful people She's put into my life. Without them I'm sure that I would have lost my way. To Elizabeth Wales, my super agent and friend, thanks a million times over for your continued belief and steady encouragement in me and my work. To Adrienne Reed, Elizabeth's assistant, for all of your supportive comments. It's so nice to hear the smile in your voice when I call. A heartfelt thanks to Carole DeSanti, my editor and friend, for recognizing my voice as a writer and encouraging me to use it. Your friendship and expertise mean the world to me. To Alex Babanskyj, Carole's assistant, for all of your helpful support. You're a whiz kid. To Zola Mumford, my assistant, for all of your loyal support. Thanks for always coming to my rescue.

To Dr. Margaret Cashman, M.D., Dr. Lynn Simkins Stone, Ph.D., Dr. Laura Brown, Ph.D., Dr. Kirk Strosahl, Ph.D., Dr. Patricia Robinson, Ph.D., and Dr. Greg Simon, M.D., your clinical teaching, guidance, and expertise over the years has been immensely valuable to me personally and professionally. Thank you for your steady encouragement and support.

To my family—the Conyers, Dunns, and Boyds, as always, your love, support, and prayers mean the world to me. I've loved you always and that will never change.

To my son and first love, Michael, you're always going to be my number one Star. I'm proud of you, boo.

To Boogie, for always being my main source of comfort and laughter.

To my sister girls, Charlotte Watson Sherman, Carletta Wilson, Jody Kim, Faith Davis, Alma Arnold, Amy Laly, Marsha Rock, Lynn Varner, Gail Myers, Brenda Freeman, Pam Asida, Fran Frazier, Wanda Laws, Donna Manier, Cheyla Axtell, Maria Root, Barbara Thomas, and to Meri Nana-Ama Danquah, and to all my other sisters, your names are imprinted on my heart. Thank you, thank you, thank you, I love you all.

To my brother friends, Aaron Swar, Lee Terry, Albert Gentles, Paul Axtell, Bob Heller, Bruce Root, Rick Simonson, and Greg Stehman, thanks for all your love and support.

To all the sisters who shared their stories with me, thank you from the bottom of my heart. This book belongs to you.

*The weeping was all of our pain—a collective wound.*

—Anita Valerio, "It's in My Blood, My Face—
My Mother's Voice, the Way I Sweat"

DEPRESSION
2

*i have cried all night
tears pouring out of my forehead
sluggish in pulse
tears from a spinal soul
that run in silence to my birth
ayyyy! am I born? i cannot peel the flesh.
i hear the moon daring
to dance these rooms.
O to become a star.
stars seek their own mercy
and sigh the quiet, like gods.*

—Sonia Sanchez,
*homegirls & handgrenades*

# CONTENTS

Dear God! I've Lost My Mind  1

Ladies Sing the Blues  11

I've Got a Feeling  31

Life Is Hard, and Other Erroneous Misconceptions  49

Beatin' the Devil out of Depression  67

A Body of Knowledge  79

The Love's Gone Wrong Blues  105

Going for the Goal  117

The Pleasure Principle  133

Show Me a Sign  141

Gradual Awakening  147

Further Information: Dealing with the Healing  153

    Symptoms of Depression  154

    Most-Asked Questions  155

Additional Reading  161

# Dear God! I've Lost My Mind

*At first I did not fight it.
I loved the suffering.
It was being alive!
I felt my heart pump the blood
that splashed my insides
with red flowers;
I savored my grief
like chilled wine.*

—Alice Walker,
*Good Night, Willie Lee,
I'll See You in the Morning*

I was scared of living, but too afraid to die. Sitting on the side of my bed I clutched the battered pillow to my breast and stared at the dust ball making a home in the corner of my bedroom. In the midst of my vague attempt to get up and ready for work fleeting thoughts raced through my head.

"I should get ready; if I don't get a move on I'll be late."

"I'm too tired. I need more sleep. I can't miss another day."

"I'm not ready for that meeting, I didn't finish my report."

"Why can't I do anything right? What's the matter with me, I must be losing my mind."

The more I thought the less I felt like going to work. My body felt like lead, and my eyes stayed trained on the dust ball as if it held some magic answer.

I was thirty years old, my thoughts racing at the speed of light, my body struggling to keep up with the demands of working full time while parenting and attending school. I was short tempered, humorless, physically and emotionally bankrupt; food refused to comfort, and sleep was my best friend but gave precious little relief. I spent twelve out of every twenty-four hours each day holding on to tears that threatened to erupt at any time. I avoided contact with family and friends, and criticizing myself and the world was my main form of conversation. In a word, I was depressed.

*Depression* is a word we carelessly toss around to describe everything from feeling disappointed about the weather to a major global crisis. But rarely, if ever, do we have a clear idea of how often depression actually affects us as individuals.

My knowledge and awareness of depression came about in a very personal way.

"What's wrong with me, Zoey, I just can't seem to get a grip."

"I don't know, sis. Maybe it's like they say, The universe is tryin' to tell you somethin'."

"Yeah! Well if that's true the message must be I'm losing my damn mind."

"You better make a house call and help her out, Lord, 'cause I think she's done lost it for sure."

Never being a devoutly religious person, I found myself resorting to prayer in a frantic need to find answers. "Dear God, please, what's happening to me?" I whispered as I watched myself spiral downward from being a cheerful go-with-the-flow type of person to being a moody, irritable, anxious person who got overwhelmed at the drop of a hat. Where I once enjoyed spending time and kickin' it with my close friends, fun now seemed like a four-letter word, w-o-r-k.

"Girl, where you been? I haven't heard from you in ages."

Tears slid slowly down my cheeks as I sat listening to the voices on the answering machine, all of them echoing the same version of my absence from their lives. I searched my thoughts for ways to respond, knowing that I wouldn't, couldn't get back to them anytime soon. Talking on the phone, usually my favorite way to stay in touch, just seemed like too much trouble. I tried to reason with myself that I was just too busy right now, but busy doing what? I was just busy feeling too lonely to connect.

"What's the matter, Mom?" I heard my son's concerned question as I stood staring vacantly out of my bedroom window thinking about all the things I should be doing and not having the energy to do any of them. I didn't answer because I didn't have an answer. How do you explain emptiness, that sensation of being physically present and emotionally distanced at the same time?

Days melted into each other as I pushed myself to complete simple mundane tasks like getting up, getting dressed, going to work, coming home, fixing dinner, and going to bed. My constantly tired state made me crave sleep like a thirsty person craves water. I knew I'd pull it together at some point—I always had in the past—but each time the mood hit it became harder to shake and with each round I found myself less willing to put up a fight.

"Sweetcakes, what you need is a good all-purpose multi-vitamin pill," Zoey offered, as I explained in guarded detail how I'd been feeling, on our Saturday drive downtown to the mall.

"Zoey, maybe I have some form of brain tumor," I said timidly as I stared out of the car window. "I mean, it's like I can't remember anything anymore."

"You been to the doctor. Did the doctor say you had a tumor?" Zoey asked as she expertly raced past an eighteen-wheeler, steering with one hand and extracting the cigarette from her mouth with the other.

"No, the doctor couldn't find anything physically wrong." I mumbled, as I rechecked my safety belt.

"Well, then, if the doctor didn't say you have a tumor, then why you stressin'."

This matter-of-fact statement seemed more than a tad bit suspicious coming from a woman who believed less in doctors than I did in magic.

Wandering up and down the aisles of the health food store, mindlessly picking up and putting down brightly wrapped bottles and packages of tonics, pills, and potions, I thought about the conversation I'd had with my doctor.

"Am I crazy?" I asked expectantly.

"No, you're not crazy," came her easy reply.

"I feel crazy." I pushed for confirmation.

"I know you feel that way, but you're not," she tried to reassure.

"Do I have some type of cancer? Maybe a brain tumor?" I fished for answers.

"Your medical chart doesn't confirm that finding, nor is there any other information that supports evidence of a brain tumor." She smiled slightly, trying to still my fears.

"Here you go, girlfriend," Zoey called out, snapping me out of my thoughts as she met me head on in aisle two, pushing her red shopping cart filled to overflowing. Staring down into Zoey's cart heaped with nerve tonics, energy boosters, and sleep enhancers, the tears I had tried to keep so carefully checked escaped down my cheeks, spilling onto the brightly colored packages, and creating a wet bleary montage of confusion.

"What's wrong with me, Doctor?" I cried softly, fearing the worst.

"From everything you've told me, all the signs point to your being clinically depressed."

While I heard my doctor's words, I wasn't ready to absorb the meaning. In fact, as she patiently explained the signs and symptoms of depression, I found myself quietly mumbling "un huh," nodding my head in agreement as I gathered up my coat and purse, giving her suspicious glances out of the corner of my eye as I prepared to make a hasty exit from her office. Clearly this doctor didn't have a clue about me, I reasoned tearfully to myself as I frantically searched the parking lot for my car. I was an intelligent, upwardly mobile, strong Black woman moving at warp speed with my future sights set on personal success. I didn't have time for petty grievances and even less time for something called depression.

I knew something wasn't right and my gut told me that my doctor's statement made sense, but my mind wouldn't allow my thoughts to wrap themselves around the belief that I might have an identifiable problem. Like the majority of people who suffer from depression, my unclear thought pattern had turned the word into a maze of totally unrelated words—instead of "depression" I heard "crazy," "lazy," "failure," and "weak." At that time in my life I didn't know what depression was, but like many of us, I had heard scary rumors.

"Don't tell nobody, but I heard the girl had a nervous breakdown."

"She's just weak spirited is all, lettin' that man walk all over her."

"She's just lazy, she just needs to get up off her behind and do some work."

I need to put on my professional therapist hat for just a moment here. Each week in my clinical practice, I encounter a significant number of sisters who present various symptoms on a clinical continuum from vague feelings of unhappiness to serious forms of physical illness, all of which include some form of depression. When presented with the assessment of depression it's not uncommon, as I myself also experienced, that there's often a period of denial during which we struggle with our thoughts and feelings surrounding our beliefs about being strong Black women, and having an illness that we've long associated with weakness of the lowest kind. I've witnessed that sisters experience a range of emotions, everything from dissolving into tears to withdrawing into complete silence, to leaving my office never to return again, at the mere mention of the word "depression." It appears that as Black women we can forgive ourselves a multitude of sins, save for one—being depressed. As Black women we want to believe that our historical lineage of survival coupled with our indomitable strength of spirit will protect us from what we consider to be a personal weakness. But we are not immune, nor is there a lack of complex life issues that contribute to the illness of depression. Raising families sometimes single-handedly, working jobs that contribute to physical and emotional stress while offering little in terms of economic survival, and trying to balance the highs and lows of relationships are just a few of the many daily issues that play a major role in the development of depression. It's been estimated by the National Institute of Mental Health that one in five women will experience depression in her lifetime, and I believe, as do other mental health professionals, that these numbers are just the tip of a very large iceberg. In fact, it's highly likely that the numbers of one in five women are pretty conservative, as they only reflect the numbers of women who actually report symptoms to their doctors. I would also venture an educated guess that we as Black women tend not to report signs and symptoms of depression, not because it doesn't impact our lives, but because we don't associate the symptoms with an illness, and therefore don't fully understand the serious impact that depression has on our overall health.

Many of us are more than a little afraid of what we don't know, and the realities of depression fall into that vague, yet tangible lack of awareness. Our fears about craziness, laziness, of being a failure or weak keep us from accepting what is true. Our fear of wearing yet another "label" attached to our ethnicity and gender as Black women has locked many of us into a state of helpless and sometimes hopeless confusion concerning our emotional well-being.

A 1997 study conducted by the National Center for Health Statistics showed by individual self report that Black women experienced depression, restlessness, boredom, loneliness, upset, and anxiety at rates three times higher than white males. While the overall objective of this study was not specifically geared to examine the happiness factor in our lives as Black women, the study does give us some interesting and important data to think about in regard to how a large number of us are coping with stress in our lives.

Several years ago I wrote a book entitled *In the Company of My Sisters: Black Women and Self-Esteem*. As a clinical psychotherapist I recognized that we operate daily under enormous stress and pressure related to economic survival, family responsibility, and social relationships that threaten our self-esteem, our ability to feel good about who we are and how we function in life. Mental health studies have proven that when self-esteem is low, depression is generally high, often interfering with our ability to take positive steps in our lives.

I found myself fearful, afraid and suspicious of my doctor's diagnosis, not because she was right, but because I didn't have information that could help me feel less vulnerable. I was even willing to risk having cancer, because on some level I thought I knew what to expect from cancer; after all, we have movies, books, and newspaper articles about cancer survivors and victims. Every year national charities gave telethons hosted by big-name celebrities to raise public awareness, and money for research; people wore ribbons to promote their support for a cure. In my depressed mind I even felt there was a level of dignity in having cancer. People knew what cancer was, I wouldn't have to explain or defend it. But most of all, and more important than anything else, I reasoned in my dysfunctional state that with cancer I wouldn't have to view myself as being weak.

My mother used to have a saying: *"You can't beat the devil you don't know."* And depression has presented itself as a devilish beast in our lives. Our misguided beliefs regarding the strength we possess in coping with stressful life situations often places us in the dangerously vulnerable position of experiencing denial when confronted with symptoms of depression. It's especially difficult to recognize how much stress we're coping with when we consider the fact that the majority of our personal and collective validation is related to our need to be perceived as strong. As one sister said to me after describing several major stressors in her life, "Are you sure I'm depressed? I thought I was just feel-ing sorry for myself."

I wasn't surprised by her remark; it had the sting of déjà vu. Depression can be seductive in its simplicity, especially when coupled with beliefs that we value as being necessary to our survival. When I asked this same sister what she knew about depression she stated:

"I heard about it and all, mostly on talk shows and stuff like that. You hear people talking about being depressed all the time, but I just think they don't have their act together. They had this doctor on one show and he was talking about depression and how taking Prozac could help you feel bet-ter and all. I thought about it for a quick minute, but then I didn't think I was as sick as all that. I mean I go to work every day, take care of my kids and all and I even take a couple of classes at the community college. I get a little down in the mouth every once in a while and feel a little blue, but I never thought that made me depressed."

"Down in the mouth," the "blues," "in a funk," "get an attitude," and "feel down"—we call it by a variety of names, but the signs are all the same and they point to depression. Many of us may never be comfortable applying the label of depression to our personal lives. As Black women we've made the discovery that naming something endows us with the power to claim it, so calling our low periods depression could prove to be dangerous, especially if it meant that we "didn't have our act together." In reality the symptoms often do mirror the stereotypes that have been projected onto Black women for years. As a people, we've also been taught to be suspicious of things that are outside of our frame of reference. This makes sense when we examine our history, especially in the area of health care. Traditionally the field of medical science has treated us like second-class citizens literally and figuratively, even with the contribu-tions and advancements that have been made by many of the world's most prominent Black physicians. Old suspi-cions have a habit of dying hard, and rightly so. Many of the corrective measures that the medical profession has taken in regard to addressing the medical needs of people of color have come a little late to gain our full sense of trust. So it stands to reason that we might be a little more than cautious when it comes to accepting and applying a medical diagnosis to a group of vague-sounding symptoms that medical professionals call *depression*. Why indeed should we accept a clinical term for something that affects our lives as Black women? In truth we don't have to accept it, nor do we have to apply it to our lives. However, it may be in our interest to examine the facts. After all, it's not the name or label that's causing us problems, it's the symptoms that do us harm.

Studies show that depression is the leading cause of mental health–related deaths (read suicide) in the United States. And we've only to look in our own back yard to see evidence of the mortally wounded. Singer Phyliss Hyman, writer Teri Jewel, and journalist Leanita McClain are but a few that have been victims of suicide caused by depression.

Phyliss Hyman was a gifted singer and Broadway performance artist. Teri Jewel was an up and coming young writer who edited a spirited book of quotations by Black women and had written short stories that appeared in several noteworthy anthologies. Leanita McClain was a talented journalist who wrote editorials for the *Chicago Tribune* and for several leading women's magazines. All were young, all gifted, all Black women, and all died by their own hand after struggling with the emotional devastation of depression. The emotional war these sisters fought, claimed their strength, silenced their creativity, and ultimately took their lives. All of these sisters left us notes telling how they felt weighed down by the world (a sense of helplessness), describing in various ways their own lack of accomplishment (a sense of failure), and their sorrow for not being able to do more (a sense of hopelessness), all of which are serious calling cards of depression. We don't know how long these sisters had been hurting, nor do we know what they called their emotional symptoms, but we do know that they died, and in my world one sister's death is one too many. When we don't have information and clear understandable facts, it becomes difficult to make choices or find solutions that will allow us to cope with the situations that confront us on a daily basis.

I was recently asked why I would want to write a book on depression directed to Black women. As a psychotherapist

I'm aware that depression is the most common mental health problem in the United States. I'm also aware that depression is one of the most treatable of all clinical emotional disorders as identified by mental health experts. As a Black woman I can relate to our "Be strong" and "Hang in there" credos for life, which often causes us to ignore, dismiss, or feel ashamed of thoughts and feelings that mimic personal weakness. As a sister I can also respect and understand our need for caution when it comes to accepting the word as gospel when it's presented by a field of science that has not always respected our needs. However as both a Black woman and a mental health professional I can't ignore the disturbing facts that as sisters we're hurting in large numbers, and the magnitude of that pain has been strong enough to cause some of us to take the most precious gift we've been given . . . our lives.

*Can I Get a Witness: For Sisters When the Blues Is More Than a Song* was written and designed with two major focuses: (1) to provide awareness and information about depression, and (2) to give witness to the belief that healing and recovery from depression is possible. I would like to state very clearly that this book is not a substitute for professional help. While it's been clinically proven that self-help methods for treating depression have been very effective for some individuals, I would strongly urge any sister who's having thoughts or feelings related to wanting to hurt yourself to please contact a professional at your nearest community mental health clinic, hospital, church, community center, or school.

For those of you who know my work from previous books, you know I never work alone, so I've included the voices of my sisters in all of their natural glory, as we discuss, agree, disagree, testify, deny, and question how the symptoms of depression impact our lives. I've also included the different faces of depression, stories from sisters whom I've met along the way who've shared their experiences as we've traveled together in search of ways to make sense of the complexities that make up the situations and feelings known as depression.

# Ladies Sing the Blues

## FAST FACTS
▼▲▼▲▼

One in five women will experience depression in her lifetime.

Women are twice as likely to suffer from depression than men.

Depression affects people of all races, ages, and social backgrounds.

Women of color may experience symptoms of depression differently due to ethnic and cultural beliefs.

Depression is not a sign of personal weakness.

## EMMA'S STORY

*I'm scared I'm having a nervous breakdown. I don't know what's wrong with me. Half the time, I don't even want to get out of bed in the morning. I just don't want to be bothered with nothing and nobody. I don't know, maybe I am crazy. I shouldn't be feeling this way. I mean, it's not like my life is all that hard: I'm thirty-five, have a good job teaching fourth graders which I love, but I don't even want to be bothered with that anymore. School just started last month and I've already missed four days, and I've been late twice. That's not like me at all. My principal called me into her office yesterday to ask if I was having problems, and I just started crying right there on the spot. What could I tell her . . . I'm okay, Miss Hayes, I'm just having a nervous breakdown right before your very eyes. This woman thought enough of my teaching skills last year to give me an honors class this year—I can't let her and those kids down. This is my big chance to prove myself and move up in the field of education.*

*My family's been great helping around the house because I just can't seem to pull it together at home either. I know they're trying to be supportive, but I just feel like I'm letting everybody, including myself, down. Sometimes I feel like such a phony and everybody—my family, my principal, and my students—are going to find out that I don't know what in the world I'm doing. As it is I already feel as if they can see right through me. I've even considered asking for my old position back, but when I talked to Morris about it, he told me not to be silly. He said it's normal to feel a little nervous when you're doing something new. I tried to explain to him, baby, this is more than just being a little nervous, I'm scared to death, but he just didn't get it. What if I blow it? I'll lose my job and everybody's respect. I just couldn't stand it if I let those kids down, they look up to me. Their parents will hate me, and I wouldn't blame them one bit because I'd hate myself too. I've been feeling this way since the first day of school, and I'm tired, I just don't want to feel like this anymore. I can't go on like this, right about now I either want to get better or I want to . . . God, I don't know what I want anymore.*

## TONI'S STORY

*I guess deep down I've always known that I was depressed.
I've never put a name to it, but the symptoms have always
been pretty clear for me. I just didn't want to deal with it, but
I've felt this way on and off since I was about twelve. That's
when my parents got a divorce and that was pretty hard on
me; actually it was hard on all of us kids (I have two older
brothers). My brothers got to live with my father, and I stayed
with my mother. She's German but my parents have always
raised us to embrace both our Black and German ethnicities.
It's just that when my father left I really felt like I had to be
Blacker than Black in order to prove myself. At school, it's
like when another Black student messes up, I feel like I have
to over-perform so that the teachers won't think we're
(Blacks) all goof-offs. I know it doesn't make sense, but I just
feel that way. It's like everything is so serious in my life,
sometimes I get on my own nerves. I've always felt that if I
gave in to my feelings of wanting to just give up, I'd be letting my father down, but lately it just seems like I can't concentrate enough to get my studies done, and I have finals
coming up in another month.*

My new rebuilt engine in my twelve-year-old used car
had just played out in the middle of Highway 167, my
son's babysitter had just informed me when I dropped him
off that she would be moving to Kansas in four weeks to be
closer to her aging mother, I had just started a new job, and
to top it all off I had a run the size of California in my last
pair of panty hose. Sitting on the bumper of my car waiting
for the tow truck with my head in my hands, I contemplated
the merits of lighting a match, tossing it in the gas tank,
and just moving on down the highway headed for places
unknown. "Look'a here, girlfriend, you know neon orange
with bold black numbers really isn't your idea of style, so
don't go stupid on us now," my gut reasoned with my overwhelmed gray matter. "I'm tired and fed up. Why can't anything ever go right for me? I'm a good person; why can't my
life just be normal like everybody else's? I can't ever do
anything right. I always screw everything up," I mumbled
to myself over and over in a tired mantra, as I sat and

waited. Needless to say, two days later I was sitting in my doctor's office watching her write out prescriptions for skin cream, asthma inhaler, and antacids, while listening to the lecture I had heard from her often.

"You've got to do something about the level of stress you've been dealing with in your life. It's wearing your body out."

"Thank you, Doctor, I will," I said, hitching my clothes up with one hand and reaching for the prescriptions with the other.

"I'm going to write down the name of somebody I think you should meet. Maybe she can help you to start managing your stress," she said as she handed me the extra piece of paper.

As I sat in the pharmacy waiting for my prescriptions I looked at the name on the piece of paper my doctor had handed me and thought to myself, well, unless she's a damn good mechanic or babysitter I really don't think there's a whole lot this lady can do for me. I politely tucked her name and number in the far recesses of my bulging purse. One month later I found myself frantically tossing the contents of my purse searching for that number as yet another series of what felt to be never-ending crises erupted in my life.

"What's wrong with me," I cried. "Am I crazy, or what?"

"You're not crazy," she said, calmly, and then went on to explain. "From the amount of stress (there was that word again) that you've been dealing with, and all the symptoms you've described—restless sleep, low energy, lack of interest in things you enjoy, general feelings of helplessness, unhappiness, and medical issues—it sounds to me as if you're experiencing a level of depression."

I can't honestly say I had never heard the word depression before; however, I had never heard it applied to me. Obviously this lady had made a mistake. Of course, that was it; she had mistaken my stuff for someone else's. I had talked to her about stress and here she was talking about depression, I mumbled to myself as I fumbled for my car keys. Going from stress to depression, now there was a leap I wasn't ready to take, I thought as I carefully navigated my brand-new rental car out of the parking lot. I told myself that I wouldn't go back, even though I had set up a return appointment, but as the week went by I found myself more and more curious as to how this doctor had come to her conclusion. I had heard about depression, and what I had heard didn't seem to fit me. Depression was a mental illness; being depressed meant that you were crazy, lazy, unmotivated, and just downright sick in the head; take your pick, any one or all of the above. I needed to go back and set this woman straight. I may deal with the blues now and then, but this sister wasn't depressed, no sir! Not this sister. On my second visit I learned depression is a complex emotional disorder with diverse symptoms and a wide range of effects on each individual it touches.

"Generally a depressed mood is triggered by an accumulation of stresses. Sometimes these are small things that tend to mount up or it could be one large overwhelming event," she explained, as I rattled off all of the problems that seemed to be bearing down on my trembling shoulders.

"How do I know I'm not crazy?" I challenged.

"Because you're not out of touch with reality," she countered knowledgeably.

"Why haven't I been depressed before now? I've been through a lot more than this," I questioned, as I thought about my divorce five years earlier.

"I have no doubt that you probably have experienced some depression in the past from everything you've told me. But you had and still have good coping skills, and what sounds like a reliable support system, so you were able to move through the depressed cycle."

I found that the more this doctor talked the more I was beginning to understand some of the mysteries of depression. She explained that depression is very common, one in five women and one in ten men will experience depression in their lifetime. She pointed out that there were four signs to look for in assessing a depressed mood.

**How you think:** Being critical of yourself and having a negative view of everything and everyone around you, past, present, and future.

"Good Lord!" I thought to myself. "How did this woman know that I'd been mentally kicking myself for not dealing

with my car problems sooner before its untimely demise."
It's true my mind's inner critic had been working overtime,
dealing with the changing child care situation, wondering
if I'd be able to take on the challenges of a new job, and
worrying about stretching my already meager budget to
cover yet one more bill.

**How you feel:** Unexplained sadness, irritability, feelings of
hopelessness, feelings of guilt.

"She hit the target again," I thought. It was true. With
each paralyzing thought about paying for needed car re-
pairs and hassling with the details of finding safe reliable
child care, I could feel my "can do" spirit sinking deeper
and deeper into the unknown.

**How you act:** Physically slowed down, isolated, and re-
moved from others.

Did this woman have spies or something? How did she
know that I had been avoiding folks? The reality was that I
felt so tired lately that I just didn't want to be bothered.

**How your body reacts:** Problems sleeping, increased or decreased eating, unexplained illness.

"That's it!" I thought. "This woman wasn't a therapist,
she was clairvoyant." I felt sleepy all the time, I hadn't had
a good night's sleep in months.

My therapist went on to explain that symptoms of depression could last anywhere from a few weeks to several
years. But the most important thing I learned was that *what
you think determines how you feel.* When I think about it
now, returning for that follow-up appointment was the best
gift I could have ever given myself. You don't need to guess
who got straight . . . it was me.

I began to understand that by having a number of stressful situations going on in my life in a short period of time
without being able to fully resolve any of them, I had worn
down my emotional reserve. After a while, worrying about
everything started to affect my mood. I found out that it was
not only the problems themselves that affected me, but also
the way in which I thought about the problems.

*Whoa, back up, sis, you just lost me on that one. What do
you mean it was the way you thought about the problem?*

*Where I come from if you have a problem you fix it and move on, end of story.*

*—Flo*

What I discovered, Flo, is that it's not always the problem that stresses us out, it's generally the way in which we think about the problem that causes us to feel stressed. For example, when my car died on the highway, my first thoughts were "I can't do anything right," "I always screw up," "Everything I do turns out wrong." The more I judged myself as being incompetent, the worse I felt. Actually, I wasn't incompetent at all. It's true my day hadn't started out very well, but that one day wasn't a reflection on my entire life. But by the time that tow truck got there I was ready to sink into the nearest hole and pull the earth right over my head.

*So what you're sayin' is that the doctor told you that you were depressed just because you were havin' a hard day. Personally I don't see what's so bad about what you were thinkin', 'cause Lord knows I would have been thinkin' the same thing. As a matter of fact I'd been wonderin' what you'd been smokin' if you said you weren't upset.*

*—Joyce*

You're right, Joyce, there's no way in the world that I could have been happy about everything that morning, that's for sure, but blaming myself didn't help the situation.

*Girl, I'm just glad it was you instead of me, 'cause see, I would have went with your first thought of blowing that sucker up.*

*—Eboni*

*I heard that, Eboni. 'Cause if the way you think makes you depressed, then I should've been seeing a doctor a long time ago. But hey, it's like this. Some things you just got to get over, so that you can keep on keepin' on, know what I mean?*

*—Flo*

There was a time when I believed that too, Flo, but I discovered that my ability to keep on keepin' on was wearing pretty thin. Since seeing my doctor, I've been doing some research and I've come across several articles on the effects of depression. In an article in one of my women's health magazines a doctor on the east coast did some research that showed people who suffer from depression tend to have very low perceptions of themselves and their self-worth. It also pointed out some of the same things that my doctor commented on, such as more women than men deal with depression because we deal with more sexual and domestic violence, financial stress, and failed relationships, which have all proven to be powerful triggers for depression. There was also some research that pointed out that Black women tend to be more unhappy with their lives than anyone else.

*Hold up! Hold up! Just a daggone minute here. You mean to tell me just because I'm a Black woman, broke, and divorced that I'm gonna be depressed too? What's up with that? Girl, if I wasn't depressed before, I sure am now.*

*—Flo*

*Child, please! Can you blame us? Just look at all the madness we got goin' on around us. Folks can't find decent jobs, babies havin' babies, young kids out there sellin' drugs and killin' one another. Yeah we're unhappy, and gonna get a whole lot unhappier if folks don't start gettin' their minds together. Now! That's my research, and I didn't need somebody on the East Coast to figure it out either. Now can I get a witness on that?!*

*—Eboni*

*Amen! Eboni, amen. Girl, I'm right here in your corner, 'cause I've been sayin' the same thing myself for years. We just got to get ourselves together. Folks just need to get right with the church and get re-involved with the community again, then we wouldn't have time to be depressed or nothing else. We don't need doctors or anybody else tellin' us what's wrong with us, we already know what's wrong and if we know what's wrong then we can make it right. I'm fifty-nine years old, and believe you me, I've seen my share of troubles—men, babies, jobs, you name it, I've been there and done that, as the kids say, but I don't think I was ever*

depressed. Now I ain't gonna deny that I've been down a
time or two, but I've always believed that you take the salt
with the sugar in life and get on with it. I've known the time
when I didn't know where my next meal was coming from,
but somehow with the Lord's help I made it through. I don't
know a whole lot about what depression is or isn't but I do
know that sometimes we just have to have a little faith and
roll with the punches. Seems like we're quick to look for excuses and reasons for every lil' thing that happens to us. And
the truth of the matter is sometimes we're just going to have
hard times.

—Queenie

Well if church is over, I'll throw my two cents in the plate. I'm
not a big fan of all this research either, but I do know that all
this crazy stuff that's happenin' with our kids out in the
streets starts somewhere, and I've said it before and I'll say it
again—I think it starts on the homefront. Now I don't know if
being depressed or havin' low self-esteem can make a young
sistah go out and get a baby, or make a brother sell drugs,
but if it does then I think all of us grown folks need to clean
up our act. Now Lord knows I grew up in a home where I
know I was loved, but that love didn't always take the form
of a Hallmark commercial, if you know what I mean. Now,
personally I don't think I deal with depression, cause I love
me to death, but I have my blue spells every now and again,
and nobody is more committed to the community than I am.
Shoot, I've even been known to make a first Sunday every
now and then.

—Zoey

Well, as for myself I know I've been depressed, and the reason I know is because my doctor told me I was, and it's like it
wasn't a big deal to me; I was just so glad to know what was
wrong, 'cause I just knew I was a goner. When Dr. Cash told
me, I was like, "Thank God, somebody knows what's going
on." It was right after I had Jamie. I was a natural-born mess,
every time lil' Jamie cried, I cried right along with him. I was
scared to death. I was only twenty years old and didn't know
the first thing about taking care of a baby—shoot, I could
barely take care of myself. James wasn't any help at all, he

*just kept telling me, you've got to pull yourself together, Lyndey, you've got to pull yourself together. But I just couldn't 'cause I didn't have a clue as to what was going on with me. It got to the point that I didn't want to hold the baby or even nurse him, 'cause it seemed like every time I even looked at him he'd start to cry. Finally we sent for Mama and honey, I can't tell you how happy I was to see her. Mama told me I just had a bad case of the nerves and she put me to bed and bless her heart she took care of me and the baby for about the first month. When I took the baby for his six-week checkup, I told Dr. Cash what had been going on with me, and he told me that I had post-natal depression and that it was pretty common in new mothers. He asked me if I wanted to take something for it. By then I was feeling better so I didn't really need any medicine. But I can tell you this, it sure helped to hear I wasn't losing my mind. I swear going through that was worse than going through those ten hours of labor. I knew I was unhappy and I knew I felt bad, but I didn't know I was depressed, but I'll tell you this, I'll know next time.*

*—Lyndey*

*Some days I feel like I'm the most fragile Strong Black Woman I know. Now that probably doesn't make much sense, but it's true. It's like I'll start off just fine and if one little thing happens it sends me into a tailspin. I forget what I'm doing from one minute to the next and I start stuff and don't finish. Half the time I can't even remember why I started doing whatever it is I'm doing. I was watching a television program the other night and this commercial came on and I started tearing up. I mean it's just plain crazy. I was sitting in a meeting the other day and I was looking dead at the presenter, but I wasn't hearing a word she was saying—it was like I was watching a movie with the sound turned off. Sometimes I think if I fell down on the floor I'd break into a million pieces. You know I was in the beauty shop the other day and this sistah was talking about how they just had to put her aunt in a home because she had Alzheimer's disease, and I got to thinking maybe that's what I have. I mean it kind of fits. Sounds kinda funny now, but at the time it seemed to make sense.*

*—Ella*

Ella, have you considered the possibility that you might be depressed? From everything you've been saying it certainly sounds like some of the signs are there. Actually, I think we've all been talking about the different ways we've been feeling and it really sounds like depression has touched most of us in one way or another. I think it's hard for us to admit to ourselves when we're stressed out and overloaded, but the reality is that we're human and there are times when we just can't handle everything no matter how strong we think we are.

*I don't think I'm there yet, sis, to be real honest. It's true I've got some stressful stuff going on right now, but depression just sounds so permanent, you know what I mean?*

*—Ella*

*I know where you're comin' from, Ella. We all get the blues every once in a while, it's no biggie, like Flo said, you do what you gotta do and move on. It's not that I don't think that people get depressed, I do, but I just don't think that it fits for us . . . you know, as Black women. And if we do get down every now and again, look at all the stuff we're dealin' with. I didn't hear where any of those big-time researchers were lookin' at things like racism or sexism; shoot, we've got that kind of stuff staring us in the face every day. If anybody can afford to be down it's Black folks. I mean, look at what our mothers and grandmothers went through in their lives and we don't hear them whining about depression. I think sometimes we just gotta put on a brave front, and go through the fire so that we'll come out a lil' stronger.*

*—Eboni*

*Well, honey, I gave up my brave front a long time ago. I remember when I came out, I was about twenty-five and in rehab. I was in group and the counselor asked us if there was anything that might make us start using again, and I started thinking about my being attracted to women. Anyway, I must have had this look on my face, 'cause she asked me what I was thinking and I started crying, 'cause I knew deep down that if I left the center that night I'd start drinking and drugging again because that was the only way I could* handle those feelings. So I told her and the group what was on my mind. My counselor told me that I did the right thing by speaking up about it, that I would probably have a lot of feelings, one of which would be depression about revealing that information, and that the group would help me deal with those feelings. Well, honey, she surely hit the nail on the head with that one, 'cause all I could think about was how my family was going to react. I already knew that I'd have to deal with the reality of being a triple target, you know, racism, homophobia, and sexism in the real world, and I didn't want to have to deal with that in my family too. I knew my family would be happy about my being clean and sober, but I didn't think they would be able to handle my being a lesbian, 'cause they're all pretty religious. As it turned out Mama just kind of accepted it, Daddy did what he always does and just pretended not to hear a mumbling word I said, but my older sister's reaction really shocked me. She threw a fit, calling me a freak, and telling me that I was a disgrace to the family. I really got super depressed after that 'cause Cheryl and I used to be so close. But that was five years ago. Now when we get together nobody talks about it. Cheryl and I talk but I get kind of sad 'cause I know we'll never be as close as we used to be. That was one of the hardest times of my life, mainly because I wasn't drugging and drinking. You all may not know this but I came real close to just callin' it quits and checkin' out of the race. It may sound kinda silly and foolish now, but back then it didn't seem like a bad idea at all. I can honestly say that going to meetings and working with my counselor, plus having you all is what keeps me going from day to day, and I'm not just talking about being clean and sober either.

—Cassie

Well now, hearin' that kind of talk troubles me, 'cause there ain't nothing out there worthy of your life. We've just got to be stronger than that. I can't speak for nobody else, and I don't want to put a whole lot of rhyme or reason to it, but when I'm really feelin' poorly I just do what I always heard my mama do. I'd just hear mama say, "Bless'd Jesus, shine your ever present light on my humble soul, in your Father's heavenly name, amen." Now I don't know why, but it works, *and I can just feel him workin' in my soul to lift the burden. Now maybe I'm old-fashion' and just don't get it, but what happen to believin' in God and believin' in yourself? If I thought about killin' myself every time something bad happen to me, I'd be dust on the road by now. You all can say what you want but I think you all have been watchin' too many of those TV talk shows. I still believe what my mama told me and what the Bible says: The good Lord just ain't gonna give you more than you can bear. Now again, maybe I'm just from the old school, but that's what I honestly believe and it ain't steered me wrong yet.*

—Queenie

*I hear you, sistah Queenie, and please believe me 'cause I mean no disrespect, but I just don't believe that God gives us depression, so therefore I don't believe it's God's job to take it away. Personally, I think God gets a little sick and tired of us waitin' on Her to take care of everything. We've got to start lookin' at ways to take care of ourselves. I mean, God looks out for us and all, and She's gonna be in our corner so to speak, but there's just some things we've got to do for ourselves.*

—Zoey

I kind of agree with you, Zoey, but I think it's hard to take care of ourselves when we aren't always aware of what's wrong with us. I was raised to believe that I was supposed to be strong and handle whatever came my way. When my depression hit, it really kind of blew me away because I just thought I was being weak. And there were times when I did blame God, not because I thought God made me depressed, but because I thought God knew how I was suffering and wouldn't help me out. Like Queenie, my religious upbringing had taught me that if you ask God for something you got it. Well, I was asking for help and I thought God was ignoring me. The more I learn about the signs of depression, the more I think it looks a lot like weakness, which might be one of the reasons we're less likely as Black women to identify it in our lives. I think we become so used to putting on a brave front that we've honestly forgotten how to evaluate the quality of our lives based on anything other than the level of struggle we have to deal with each day. However I agree with you I don't believe that God gives us depression as a test of human endurance, to see if we're "strong enough" to handle life.

I also believe that a large part of the problem is that we just don't know enough about depression and the impact it has on our lives. While we can't ignore the reality of the issues that Eboni talked about, as far as how we've been overlooked and ill treated by society at large, it doesn't divorce us from the fact that depression does affect our lives as Black women. As much as we profess to be strong, some of us are dying because there's still a lot of shame and guilt in the Black community around having an illness that's connected to our mental or emotional well-being. Let's face it, some of us are still coming to terms with the fact that Black folks have gotten and still continue to get AIDS. It took a national basketball star admitting that he was HIV positive before we were even willing to acknowledge that yes, this does happen in our community. When I think about my own skepticism when my doctor told me I was depressed, I'm not surprised that it's taking us so long to recognize that depression affects our lives too. I also believe that we've become real good at covering our emotional hurt and unhappiness with other things, like anger, drugs, alcohol, food, sex, and even prayer at times. I discovered that depression is more than just having a case of the blues. Depression is a complex mood disorder that can be triggered by any number of life stresses such as unresolved grief, serious illness, failed relationships, money problems, alcohol or drug abuse, work problems, childhood trauma, genetic predisposition, and other major losses. When these types of stresses erupt in our lives and are coupled with the pressures of daily life experiences it causes a shift in our thinking and mood. When we're confronted with major life stresses our thinking becomes overwhelmingly negative and our mood goes into a downward spiral, which triggers depression. Having adequate coping skills and a good support system very often will help us to cycle out of the depressed stage within a few days or at the very most, a couple of weeks. When our coping skills break down, and our support systems are limited, we often find ourselves entrenched in a cycle of depression which continues to deplete our emotional and physical energy and makes it difficult to get back on track.

*You know, I've been sitting here thinkin'. If what you say is true, then maybe, just maybe, I've been depressed before, but I've never really thought about it like that. I just thought, oh well, it's one of those days, or I'll get over it, and nine times out of ten I do. If I had thought about it in terms of being depression maybe I wouldn't have gotten over it so fast. I mean I'm kinda in the middle of all of this 'cause I don't care what you call it as long as I know what to do when it happens. I have my up and down days, lately they've been more down than up, but that's because things have been so crazy at work. I'm generally a person that can go with the flow, but now it's like I have so much to do and so little time to do it, but I know the pressure will ease up at some point, it always does.*

*—Joyce*

*I know I get moody from time to time, but I just chalk it up to my mother's blood, 'cause honey, she was one hard lady to read. You didn't know from one minute to the next what to expect from her. Lately though, I know I've been kind of moody 'cause we've been dealing with reorganizing in our company and folks are gettin' laid off right and left. Half the time I'm scared to open my paycheck 'cause I just know there's going to be a pink slip staring me in the face. I just bought a brand-new car, and yesterday the dentist told me that Candi, my daughter, is gonna need braces. Gettin laid off right about now would put a real hurtin' on me. I've got a little put by in the bank, but I need that steady every-two-week paycheck to keep it there, know what I mean? The way I see it, gettin' the blues every once in a while is something we've all got to deal with, and I deal with it the best way I know how. I just go and pour myself a taste of good old Johnny Walker Black, throw my Marvin Gaye CDs in the stereo, and wait for the feelin' to pass. By the time Marvin gets to "Sexual Healin' " I'm on my last drop of scotch, I fall in the bed, go to sleep, and by the time I wake up I'm good to go again. Now if you want to call that depression then go right ahead, you can slap whatever label on it you want, but I've found my cure; I can't swear it'll work for everybody but it sure works for me.*

*—Flo*

It's not that I want to call it *depression*, or slap a label on anything, it's just that I get concerned that we might be overlooking an important health issue in our lives. You all know me well enough to know that I'm not a big fan of labels and stereotypes, but I think this is something that we need to pay attention to for health reasons. Maybe we're invested in seeing ourselves as being strong Black women for all the wrong reasons, especially when our health is at stake.

*It's not so much that I'm invested in seeing myself as a strong Black woman, as it is that seeing myself as a mentally ill Black woman turns me off. Every time I pick up a newspaper and read where some lunatic has shot up a bunch of people, or some woman has seduced a fourteen-year-old kid, they say the reason for their behavior is depression. Now the paper is calling them depressed, but I'm reading crazy, and that's not me. Even with all this research I just have a hard time trusting all this medical mumbo jumbo.*

*—Ella*

*I consider myself a strong Black woman, and I don't care who knows it. Shoot, the way things are in this crazy, screwed-up world we live in, we better be strong or die, and I just ain't ready to go there yet, know what I mean? If feeling down every now and again is the only price I have to pay for standing up for myself, then I'm willing to pay the cost of being the boss. What's the alternative? I don't look good wearing nobody's footprints on my back, which is what happens when we let our guard down.*

*—Eboni*

I personally don't think that we have to give up being "strong" in order to deal with our emotional well-being. However, I'm aware that as Black women we've been given the message countless times that we're "strong" and can therefore handle anything that's put on our emotional plates. We're good at "looking good," but often the public face we wear hides an overwhelming amount of personal pain. We've got to be willing to question the presence of stress in our lives in order to preserve our emotional well-being.

*You can do it, don't ever let me hear you say that you can't do something again. You can do anything you put your mind to, always remember that.* Can't *is a word that we don't use in this house.*

I can still hear my father's words of not-so-subtle encouragement ringing in my ears as I childishly whined, making feeble excuses about not being able to complete what felt like an impossible task to my seven-year-old brain. My father's message was well intended and it served its purpose in fostering my belief that there wasn't anything that I couldn't do if I put my mind to it. As I've grown to adulthood I've found myself at times feeling blessed because of Daddy's message—the belief that I can do anything has helped me to weather many stormy times. However, I also recognize that this same message, even with its good intent, has thrown me into the depths of my own personal hell as I traveled through life encountering obstacles that were truly out of the range of *I can do* territory. Growing up empowered with the message that I was a "strong Black woman," I learned to believe that there was supposed to be nothing beyond my capabilities to master and control. The stresses came unexpectedly: divorce, the challenges of single parenting, going back to school and working two jobs. And along with the stress and pressure, depression came like a thief in the night, robbing me of my most prized possession, my *"I can do"* sense of self confidence. My fear that I had somehow failed the "strong Black woman test" pushed me deeper into myself. I put myself on trial, acting as judge and jury, using vague evidence based on my inability to be "strong" enough to handle and fix the situation. I found myself guilty as charged and the stiff sentence of emotional imprisonment was enforced. I too had learned to wear the mask of survival. I didn't want or need others to know that I was a hostage to my own beliefs. Over the years as I became more invested in my self-care, I became aware that my misery had a name—depression. Like my sisters, my inability to recognize my stress and thus my depression was based in my fear of being seen as "weak." However, as I learned more about the things that contributed to my depressed state, I discovered that I didn't have to sacrifice my sense of personal strength in public or private.

## Mood Chart

Our mood often changes several times a day but we're unaware of the changes because we generally don't pay attention. This exercise will help you to recognize the various shifts in your daily mood. For the next week, using the mood rating scale and chart on the following page, rate your mood three times a day, in the morning, at midday, and in the evening. Changes in events or situations will often trigger a shift in our mood, so it's important to pay close attention and record these two items, for example:

### Mood Rating Scale

$$1 \longleftarrow 5 \longrightarrow 9$$

|  | LOW | OKAY | PLEASANT |
|---|---|---|---|

| **Monday** | **Mood** | **Event** | **Thought** |
|---|---|---|---|
| A.M. | 2 | Late getting up | I'll be late for work |
| midday | 5 | Took a walk | I like being outdoors |
| P.M. | 7 | Movie with friend | I had a nice time tonight |

This exercise will give you a very concrete journal of just how often your mood changes throughout the day. You may also find some surprises in knowing how certain events may trigger certain thoughts. Often people are surprised to discover that even on a bad day their mood wasn't low all day, or you may notice that out of a week you only had three really low periods and most of the time you felt okay. In recording your mood you'll notice that the mood chart doesn't list "high" or "happy." That's because being undepressed doesn't necessarily mean that you'll feel happy.

In fact, most people describe their feeling as somewhere in the range of "okay" or "pleasant" when not feeling low or depressed.

| | Mood | Event | Thought |
|---|---|---|---|

**MONDAY**

| | | | |
|---|---|---|---|
| A.M. | | | |
| Midday | | | |
| P.M. | | | |

**TUESDAY**

| | | | |
|---|---|---|---|
| A.M. | | | |
| Midday | | | |
| P.M. | | | |

**WEDNESDAY**

| | | | |
|---|---|---|---|
| A.M. | | | |
| Midday | | | |
| P.M. | | | |

**THURSDAY**

| | | | |
|---|---|---|---|
| A.M. | | | |
| Midday | | | |
| P.M. | | | |

**FRIDAY**

| | | | |
|---|---|---|---|
| A.M. | | | |
| Midday | | | |
| P.M. | | | |

**SATURDAY**

| | | | |
|---|---|---|---|
| A.M. | | | |
| Midday | | | |
| P.M. | | | |

**SUNDAY**

| | | | |
|---|---|---|---|
| A.M. | | | |
| Midday | | | |
| P.M. | | | |

# I've Got a Feeling

## FAST FACTS
▼▲▼▲▼

Feelings are clouded by depression.

Feelings have a beginning, middle, and ending point.

Thoughts trigger feelings.

Feelings don't operate in a vacuum.

## HATTIE'S STORY

*I hate my job. I know* hate *is a strong word but it's really how I feel. It seems like the more I do, the more they want. I've been with the company for ten years and I just can't seem to get ahead. I work my fingers to the bone and for what? If it wasn't for a shame I'd quit. I know I'm good at what I do, and that's the only thing that keeps me going. My supervisor is always telling me that I do good work, and she's even encouraged me to try for different positions, but it's like what's the use? I mean, why get my feelings hurt applying for an upgrade when they'll just go and hire somebody else? I've thought about asking for a transfer, or even going with another company, but that would mean starting all over again, and I'm forty years old. Besides, it would just mean dealing with the same old crap in a different place. It ticks me off that a lot of people in my department do just enough to get by and they're always complaining about being overworked. I do the work of two people, and it's done right, but it's not like anybody ever really notices. Sometimes I'm so tired when I get home I can't see straight, but I keep on going 'cause I know everybody's counting on me. I haven't taken a sick day in Lord knows when, and there are days when I should have been home in bed, but I can't count on them to get my work done, and even if they did I'd only have to do it over again. I've even taken work home just so I could get it done and in on time. I dread getting up in the morning and going in, 'cause I know it's going to be the same old thing. I don't even look forward to the weekends like I used to, because I worry about what's going to be on my desk Monday morning. I feel stuck and I know I'm in a rut, but I don't have a choice—I've got to eat and keep a roof over my head.*

> I feel like eat'n some greens for dinner. Who feels
> like going to the store with me to get some?
> —Momi

Feeling language was spoken a lot in my house as a child. "It feels like it's gonna rain;" "I feel like I'm coming down with something;" "It feels to me like you all want to go to bed early, if you don't stop all that noise." Mama, my grandmother, could predict the temperature within twenty degrees one way or the other just by the feel of her bunion or a chill in her bones, which usually meant rain for sure, and we were bundled up accordingly. As I think about it feelings were pretty much the national language in our household. Weather was predicted, sleepiness was gauged, hunger was attended to and illness was warded off all based on my mother's or grandmother's ability to feel. So it's no accident of the universe that I came by my ability to use feeling language with natural ease. I would rely on my feelings to tell me what clothes to wear, what food to eat, and even what shoes to buy. I had learned to trust my feelings like most folks trust money in the bank: I could count on them come rain or shine. Like my mother and grandmother I had learned the art of predicting the states of my inner and outer worlds based solely on sensory perception alone. I feel, therefore it must be true, was my unspoken claim to fame. That is, until I entered the confusing and clouded world of depression.

"What are you thinking?" my doctor asked, interrupting the loud silence between us.

"I just feel like nothing makes sense anymore," I whispered as if talking to myself.

"Is that a thought or a feeling?" She prodded gently for clarification.

"Excuse me?" I looked up, not quite understanding the question.

"I asked what you were thinking."

"I feel like nothing I do ever turns out right anymore."

"So you're *thinking* you're a failure?"

"Yeah, I guess so. I feel like no matter what I do, it's never good enough."

"You *think* that nothing you do is adequate."

"Uh huh." I nodded my head slowly, noticing the change in her wording as she responded to my statements.

"I'm aware that you think of your thoughts as feelings, which is something people tend to do when they're depressed," she stated quietly, after I pointed out what I had noticed.

"What's the difference?"

"Well, feelings are sensory, and thoughts are cognitions," she responded playfully, and then went on to explain, "A cognition is how and what we think, and feelings are based on physical sensations. We use our thoughts and feelings to process different types of information, but often we make the mistake of believing that our thoughts are processed through our feelings, and actually it's the other way around."

Feeling thoroughly confused, or thinking that I was, and not being sure which, I decided to listen out of pure curiosity.

"Our mind is the most powerful part of our body; we use our minds to store and process all types of old and new information. But depression clouds our thoughts, giving us a form of tunnel vision which makes it difficult to process information accurately."

"What type of information do we process? What do you mean by tunnel vision? Are you saying that something's wrong with my thinking? How do you know my feelings aren't real?" The questions tumbled from my lips in my search for answers that I could hold on to.

"Our thoughts are one of the ways by which we process information about ourselves and our world, and when we're depressed the thoughts or information that we have is, for the most part, negative. Depression acts like a tunnel in that it narrows our scope of vision, only allowing the negative thoughts to pass through. When we're depressed we generally have a larger number of negative thoughts. Our thoughts and feelings process different information; however, they are connected. Sensory information passes through our thoughts, and if we're depressed then our feelings are going to be reflective of the depression."

*Girl, I must be thick, 'cause I'm still confused by all that.*

*—Flo*

Don't worry, Flo, it took me a while to get it too. But maybe I can help you by showing you an exercise that my therapist had me do. It helped me to understand it a little better.

Get comfortable in your seat and close your eyes. Now take three deep slow breaths in through your mouth and slowly release the air out through your nose. Let your body relax and clear your mind of all thoughts. Now picture a time you were in a situation that made you laugh. What were you doing? Who was with you? Hold that thought for a minute because I want you to take in all the details. Now take a deep breath and let that thought go. Now I want you to picture yourself in a situation that made you angry. What was happening? What did you do? Hold that thought for a minute. Now take a deep breath and let that go. Okay, take another deep breath, count to three, and open your eyes. Now, what did you notice?

*I remembered the time my daddy was teaching me to drive in his old pickup truck. He loved that old beat-up truck, and I didn't know what I was doing so I kept stripping the gears. Anyway I got on the freeway by mistake, and I knew poor Daddy stomped a hole in the floor on the passenger side 'cause he just kept sayin' "Stay calm, baby, stay calm," and every time he'd say it, he'd stomp his foot down like he was puttin' on brakes. We still laugh about my driving lesson when I go home to visit.*

*—Cassie*

*I thought about the time I went to church with a pair of pantyhose clingin' to the back of my dress. Child I was struttin' my stuff that Sunday, and heard the people in back of me laughing when I went to sit down. After service, Sis' Thomas came up and pretended to pat me on the back, and she pulled the pantyhose off my dress, balled 'em up, and tried to slide 'em in my hand. But when I looked down to see what she was givin' me, I almost fell out. We all just started bustin' up. I know the pastor thought we were crazy, laughin' like that in front of the church an' all.*

*—Queenie*

*I couldn't think of anything funny, but when you said something about gettin' mad I thought about my new silk blouse, 'cause I went to pull the tag off and snagged it good. Now I have to have it fixed before I can even wear it. I hate when I do dumb stuff like that.*

*—Flo*

*I couldn't think of anything either way, so I just thought about all the work I've got sitting on my desk waitin' to be done.*

*—Ella*

*Well I'm with you on this one, Ella, 'cause I was busy wondering what the point of all this was gonna be. Then I started thinkin' about what I was gonna fix to eat when I got home this evening cause all this thinkin' was makin' me hungry.*

*—Zoey*

When I did this exercise I could see the power of my thoughts. Just by being asked to recall an incident we can produce the thought and—you all might have noticed this too—not only did you have the thought, you had feelings about the thought. The doctor was right. Our feelings don't operate independently of our thoughts. We have thoughts and feelings all the time but we don't always notice how our thought process affects our feeling state.

*I don't know that I agree with your doctor, sis, cause my feelings don't usually fail me, know what I mean? When my ex was messin' around on me, I could honestly feel somethin' wasn't right. And he just kept tellin' me I was crazy, but I could just feel it in my bones that somethin' was goin' on. If I hada followed my mind I woulda still been trying to believe him when he was tellin' me all those bald-faced lies about how much he loved me.*

*—Eboni*

*I listen to my feelings too, Eboni. When my feelings tell me something I sit up and pay attention, 'cause I ain't never known them to lie. And besides, you know what they say—if you feel like something is wrong, you're probably right.*

*—Lyndey*

I don't think we should ignore our feelings either, it just makes sense to me to check them out every once in a while. I kind of like the idea that I can have more than one way to check something out. The other night is a good example. I've been having some work done on my house and there aren't any lights in the back rooms. I had fallen asleep when I heard this big crash. My first thought was Oh, my God! Somebody's broken in. Then a split second later I heard Boogie whimpering and I knew he'd gotten up and went exploring in the back rooms and knocked something over. Before I had the facts I thought someone had broken into my house and I was terrified, but after I heard my dog I knew that he had just gotten into something, and my feelings went from being terrified to being more concerned.

*Honey, if I heard a crash in the middle of the night in my house, dog or no dog, I'm history. The police would have to collect the facts later, 'cause my only feeling is gonna be my feet burnin' up the concrete on I-five.*

*—Flo*

*Flo, you need to hush. If you wasn't such a big devil during the day, you wouldn't have to worry about something being after your butt at night.*

*—Queenie*

*You know, sis, I see your point, but I see Flo's point too. I mean, half the time I don't know what I'm thinking, and I can't say that my feelings have been much better. To be honest, I don't trust either one, thinking or feeling, too much lately. Most of the time I do good just to make it from point A to point B, let alone know what I'm thinking or feeling. Anyway, it's not like thinking happy thoughts is gonna make me feel happy. If anything I would probably feel worse 'cause I'd feel like I was faking it.*

*—Ella*

I understand what you're saying, Ella. When you're overwhelmed and stressed out it's hard to distinguish your thoughts from your feelings and then put them into words. You're not alone in that respect. I believe that most of the time when we're overwhelmed or stressed out it's hard to find the words we want or need to express ourselves. I also think that as women we've become so accustomed to paying attention to our feelings that it's difficult for us to separate out our thoughts from our feeling state.

I have this theory that as women we've grown up hearing

and learning the language of feelings. In fact, we've learned the art of speaking in feeling language so well—"I feel the couch would look better in the corner," "I feel the red dress looks better on me"—that over the years we've unconsciously learned to associate feeling language with our gender, as in, "Women who speak in this way are more sensitive and feminine." Women who step outside of these perceptions are judged harshly, and often socially penalized for being "too direct," or seen as "too aggressive," which are considered to be more masculine traits. It's my belief that many of us make the unconscious decision to remain within the safe boundaries of substituting and disguising our thoughts in order to avoid being judged as unfeminine. As Black women I think we encounter a double threat when it comes to our feelings, because we're often judged by others in our community as being weak when we show or express the softer side of our emotions, and cold, distant, or stoic when we choose not to express some of our softer feelings openly. While we learned to speak in feeling language as children, we also learned that as adults, in order to be taken seriously, we've had to put aside our feelings in order to survive.

Once, after being verbally assaulted and threatened with bodily harm by a drunken vagrant as I walked through a city park, the officer on the scene told me that I didn't look as if I was too shaken up by the incident. When I asked him what he meant, he replied calmly, "Well, you know, miss, most women might have gotten hysterical, but you look as if you've got it all under control." I assured him that the absence of any emotional outburst had very little to do with how I was actually feeling at the moment. While we've grown up learning to speak the language of feelings, I think on some level it's understandable at times that we view it as unsafe to express how we're feeling in many situations. We've learned to close off the part of ourselves that would make us vulnerable in the face of others, and we've learned the lesson so well that many of us have even closed off many of those feelings to ourselves. In certain situations I had learned to address my thoughts as feelings in order to be heard, and not be judged as being too confrontational. In a strange way I had gotten out of touch with

my softer sensory feelings, feelings like happiness, pleasure, contentment, and peace, not because I didn't have
them, but because I had difficulty translating those feelings
into thoughts.

*Hold up, sis, you want to break all that down and run it by
me again? You're saying that because we're women we have
to think and feel in a certain way.*

*—Zoey*

We don't have to, Zoey, but I believe that we do it anyway.
Now this is just my theory, mind you, but when we talk in
feeling language we're seen as being more accessible and
less threatening, more feminine.

*Now that makes sense, 'cause I was reading this article that
said Whitney Houston was startin' to act like a diva cause
she was makin' all kinds of demands on her last movie
set. Now, to my way of thinkin' this sistah has more than
earned her props, and just because she starts tellin' folks
what she wants, they're gonna start dissin' her.*

*—Cassie*

*When you were talking I was thinkin' about our last produc-
tion meeting at work, and I noticed that when we go around
the table pitching ideas, it's rare to hear anybody say "I
feel." There's three men and two other women besides myself and we always use the term "I think."*

*—Joyce*

*Well, I learned early on that you could catch more flies with
sugar than with vinegar, and if it takes talkin' about my feelings to do it then I don't have a problem with that. It don't
bother me none to talk about how I'm feelin'. If I'm feelin'
fine, I'm gonna say that and if I'm feelin' poorly I'm gonna
say that too. I don't say it 'cause I'm a woman, Black or
otherwise, I say it 'cause it's true.*

*—Queenie*

*I don't always say what I'm thinkin' 'cause if I did, I'd be
in jail or pushin' up daisies right about now. 'Cause if I*

*told them how I feel, or, excuse me, what I think down at that job, I would have been fired a long time ago. So maybe you're right about it not always being safe to speak your mind, but I don't think I'm confused about which is which.*

*—Lyndey*

*I was just thinkin' I'm not so sure that I don't mix up my thoughts and feelins'. How would I know the difference?*

*—Joyce*

Here's a little trick I use to keep me straight, Joyce: If something registers in my head it's a thought, if it's in my body it's a feeling. It takes some practice at first, but I found that feelings generally register pretty strongly in my body, like tightness in the chest, fluttering in the stomach, or a tight feeling in my muscles. I also noticed that my thoughts tend to be more in words, but when I'm anxious I usually see a picture of something bad happening in my mind.

*What if they both happen at the same time?*

*—Joyce*

*Yeah, like the other night, I got off work and my car wouldn't start, so I had to walk downtown to catch a bus and it started raining. Just as I got up to the corner I saw Zoey across the street walking towards Madison Avenue, and I called hello, but you just kept walking, Zoey, just like you didn't even hear me. I really got kinda ticked. I've been meaning to ask you what was up with that, 'cause I was really feelin' kind of put out, but then my bus was comin' so I had to run to catch it.*

*—Eboni*

*Gosh, Eboni, I'm sorry. I thought I heard somebody call out but it was dark and I was coming from a city budget meeting and had a lot on my mind. You know I wouldn't diss you like that, girlfriend.*

*—Zoey*

*Yeah, when I got on the bus I kinda figured that maybe you didn't see me, 'cause it's not like you not to speak. But at the time it happened, I was kinda hurt.*

—*Eboni*

That's a perfect example of what I was talking about, Eboni. When you *felt* that Zoey was ignoring you, you were angry and hurt. But when you *thought* about it again while you were on the bus your feelings changed. It might have felt like both things were happening at once, but it sounds like you noticed your feelings first because they came through stronger and then you noticed your thoughts when things had calmed down and you felt different.

*You mean to tell me that just by thinking about Zoey not see-ing her, Eboni would feel better?*

—*Flo*

Eboni didn't feel better, Flo, she felt different when she thought about the situation. When we're in stressful situa-tions and we depend on our feelings as our first line of rea-soning the situation takes on emotional overtones. Eboni went from feeling angry to feeling hurt, those are two differ-ent feeling states. Being able to give ourselves time to think through a situation gives us a little more emotional distance.

*Well, now, I don't know about that because when something pushes my buttons, I get one serious attitude, and the more I think about it the madder I get.*

—*Flo*

*I hear you, Flo, 'cause I'm the same way myself. You know what they say, If you think long you think wrong.*

—*Ella*

Giving ourselves some emotional distance from a situa-tion can allow us to think through the situation. Personally I don't think there's anything wrong with anger; in fact there are times when anger is an appropriate response. However, in order to handle anger appropriately I may need to think through the situation. I can take on a very serious attitude, but I also recognize that I don't want my anger or attitude to govern my life. I've learned for myself that sometimes an attitude that goes unchecked for too long can quickly turn into a bad mood. Being able to step back from my anger allows me to check my attitude and allows me to make a choice as to how I want to handle my feelings. I think we have to remember that our feelings aren't facts, our feelings just give us an emotional reading.

*I learned to talk about my feelings in rehab and I think it's the best lesson I ever learned. Now I don't go around stuffin' everything down inside, and trying to numb myself out with alcohol. Talkin' about how I feel on certain things gives me a kind of freedom that for the most part helps me to feel good, know what I mean? When I talk about how I feel it gives me the power to talk about what I think. Now that might sound backwards, but it's like Flo said before, it works for me, and when somethin' works you don't mess with it.*

—Cassie

*I'm with you, Cassie, if it ain't broke don't fix it. If I can get my thoughts across by talkin' about my feelings, so be it. I like the idea of havin' choices, though, and if somethin' like standing back from my feelin' gives me a choice I'm willin' to go that route too. I guess in my case it'll depend on what I'm dealin' with at the time. But I think you all know me well enough to know that I generally don't have a problem sayin' what's on my mind one way or another.*

—Zoey

*I think one of the reasons I don't mess with my feelings too much is because if I ever let them go I'll just explode. Not in a mad way or anything, but more in the sense of being out of control. I remember when I was little these big girls at school used to tease me all the time, calling me names like tar baby and stupid stuff like that. They'd run me home crying every day. I was scared to fight those kids because they were bigger than me. One day my mother told me that I better not come in that house crying anymore or she'd give me something to really cry about. She told me that I better stand up to those girls or I'd be running for the rest of my life. Anyway, we used to carry bookbags back then and my older brother,*

*Joey, told me to put some big rocks in my bookbag and when those girls started after me, he told me to just start swinging. And honey, that's just what I did. The next day on my way to school I stopped and picked up every big rock I could find, and I filled that bag up. After school I waited for those girls, and honey when they came after me I started turning around in a circle swinging that bookbag full of rocks. I was turning, swinging, and hollering as loud as I could. I got so worked up until I made myself sick for two days, and I got suspended from school a whole week for fighting. Mama was right though, once I stood up for myself those girls didn't bother me anymore. But I still remember how I felt, so scared and out of control. That feeling scared me as much as those girls did, and I guess I never really got over how awful it felt being out of control like that. Ever since then I promised myself I'd never get out of control like that again. To be honest, my feelings scare me, so I just don't deal with them.*

—*Ella*

I believe that anger and rage are two of the feelings that we're most likely to acknowledge and accept in ourselves for a variety of reasons. As Black women, historically we've had to utilize our individual and collective anger in order to survive hardships and injustices of all kinds. Like Ella, many of us were as children given the strong message by our parents that it was important for us to "fight back whenever we felt threatened": *"You better stand up for yourself. You better not ever let me hear that you didn't fight back."* The message from our parents was clear: we had to be tough in order to survive. For many of us, being tough, or "angry," and fighting back is the only way we know how to deal with the world at large. We're all familiar with the "bad-ass sistah who don't take no stuff off of anybody" image that has earned us the negative stereotype of being "angry Black women." Even though we've been given the message and the stereotype, many of us aren't always comfortable being defined in that way, nor is it necessarily fair to expect that we can or want to live up to that image. Having to believe or feel that we have to live up to an image that doesn't fit can create its own form of stress, and again, it affects our mood in a negative way. Ella, your mother wanted you to get angry enough to fight back, which you did, but at what price? . . . You were suspended from school, and the feeling of being so angry made you sick.

*Sis, is this another one of your theories?*
*—Zoey*

Yeah, Zoey, I guess it is.

*Lord, the child's got more theories than she's got shoes.*
*—Queenie*

That may be true to Queenie, but it's like I said before, I don't think anger is a bad or unacceptable feeling. It's how we think about and use the anger that causes us problems. Anger is just like any other emotion that we have access to, it's just that we've got to start recognizing that all of our thoughts and feelings have an equal amount of strength in our lives. If we only accept one feeling as having weight and we're afraid of that feeling, then we view ourselves as powerless, and depression feeds off of feelings of power-lessness.

Feelings aren't good, bad, right, wrong, or evil, they're just feelings—nothing more and nothing less. We don't have to be afraid of our feelings, nor do we have to worry about losing control over how we feel, even when we feel our worst. It doesn't last forever. Our feelings have a begin-ning, middle, and ending, but sometimes the situations we find ourselves in are so emotionally loaded and our feelings are so intense that it's difficult to pinpoint when they start and stop. But it's important to remember that just like the feelings started, they will stop.

*My thing is that sometimes I get so stressed out till I don't know what I'm feeling from one minute to the next. It's like they get all jumbled up or somethin', I know I'm havin' feelin's but I just don't know what they are. The other day is a good example. My supervisor asked me to work overtime, and Lord knows we need the money. I wanted to say yes, but I just couldn't 'cause James was out of town, and Jamie needed to be picked up from day care, and everybody else was at work. I was stressin' hard, 'cause I knew that sayin'*

*no to overtime might make them think that I didn't want my*
*job or somethin' and they might lay me off for sure, but I*
*knew my baby had to come first.*

—Lyndey

I found it really interesting to learn that as jumbled and scrambled as our situations might be at any given time, our feelings generally tend to fall in one of four areas: *mad*, *sad*, *glad*, and *afraid*. These four areas are primary or basic feelings and depending on the situation we're in we can experience one or a possible combination of these feelings. I also found that, again depending on how much stress or pressure we're under at the time, we can experience different levels of these four feelings. For example the other day the weather was really nice so I decided to wash my car in the driveway. I was also expecting an important phone call, so I left the door slightly open so that I could hear it ring. Just as I was in the midst of untangling the water hose to rinse the soap off the car, I heard the long-anticipated ring, so I sprinted across the driveway, stumbled up the steps, snatched the screen door open, and dove for the ringing phone. I picked it up just in time to hear the dreaded click of a disconnect on the other end. Now, I don't have to tell you the thoughts that passed through my head, but I can say I experienced several stages of one particular feeling. I was mad on three different levels: angry (high) "Oh *blank*, they hung up," frustrated (medium) "I can't believe I missed it," and annoyed (low) "Oh, well, they'll call again," at missing the connection. Just like anything else in our lives our feelings have levels of intensity, which range from high to medium and low.

*What about feeling happy, I wouldn't mind just being happy*
*every now and then. But even when I'm feeling good, it's not*
*like I'm really happy anymore. Sometimes when I see little*
*kids playing and stuff I find myself wanting to be like them,*
*you know, not having any worries, or cares. And then to top*
*it all off I feel guilty because I feel so unhappy. It's like I said*
*before, my life isn't all that bad, I should be satisfied, in fact*
*compared to a lot of folks out there my life looks pretty damn*

*good. I even feel bad for talking about it out loud. But still and all I can't help but wish I was happier.*

*—Ella*

I don't think it's unreasonable to want to be happy, Ella, but I believe that we might have to redefine what happiness can be for us as adults. When we're depressed it dulls our thoughts and our feelings, so it's hard to really define happiness in a way that has meaning for us. It may be unrealistic to think that as adults we'll have the carefree feelings that children have, because as adults we're dealing with adult issues. Working, managing households, and juggling various commitments takes a lot of energy; depression saps a lot of our mental and physical energy; and so we automatically go into converse mode, which means we cut out most if not all of the activities that bring us pleasure. Fun becomes a four letter word, *w-o-r-k*, because we feel so run down and out of sorts. Even when we do allow ourselves a little pleasure, we can't enjoy it and in truth we may not even recognize the pleasure because we're busy worrying about what we should be doing. In order to experience a sense of happiness or pleasure it's important to balance our work with pleasure so that we can have a more even mood.

## Oh, Those Feelings

Oh, those feelings, they come and go in a flash. Sometimes we acknowledge them, and sometimes we don't, but our feelings are always present. We're more likely to notice extreme feelings such as being wildly excited or terribly sad, but very often we ignore those middle-of-the-road feelings like being calm or just okay. Feelings themselves aren't good or bad; however, the intensity of certain feelings (especially the sad and angry ones) often can impact our mood to a major degree. This exercise will provide you with more information regarding feeling states and help you to pay attention to all your feelings, not just the extremes. First it's important to know a little something about feelings, like the fact that there are only four primary feeling groups: **Sad, Glad, Mad,** and **Afraid,** and within each of these groups there's a range of feelings such as high, medium, and low. These feelings also occur on a continuum depending on the situation or event, for example: "I'm shocked that it happened like this, so suddenly; I'm hurt that he didn't tell me sooner." "Shocked" in this situation would be on the high end of the **afraid** continuum, and feeling *hurt* would be on the low end of the **sad** continuum.

### Feeling Continuum

Low end ◄———————Medium————————►High end

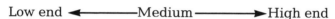

Study the list of primary feelings on the next page, noticing the group and range of feelings that you experience most often. Now think of a situation in which you've recently noticed the presence of your feelings. Using the feeling continuum think about the intensity of feeling that you experienced in that situation. Try asking yourself at least three times a day "How am I feeling?" Notice if your feelings change from hour to hour, and whether they are more or less intense at certain times of the day. You may find that you want to add other feelings to the list. Be sure to add them under a primary feeling group and give the feeling a specific intensity. Remember, your feelings aren't facts, they are feelings!

## GLAD

| High | Medium | Low |
|---|---|---|
| Excited | Satisfied | Relieved |
| Happy | Grateful | Contented |
| Cheerful | Blessed | Comfortable |
| Hopeful | Optimistic | Peaceful |
| Delighted | Playful | |
| Elated | Tickled | |

## MAD

| High | Medium | Low |
|---|---|---|
| Angry | Disgusted | "Teed off " |
| Hostile | Frustrated | Miffed |
| Enraged | Incensed | Annoyed |
| Irate | Disturbed | Peeved |
| Furious | Fuming | |
| | Bitter | |

## SAD

| High | Medium | Low |
|---|---|---|
| Empty | Blue | Distant |
| Depressed | Unhappy | Hurt |
| Hopeless | Down | Gloomy |
| Helpless | Pessimistic | Pensive |
| Numb | Ashamed | Troubled |
| Rejected | Lonely | |
| Worthless | Discouraged | |
| | Distressed | |

## AFRAID

| High | Medium | Low |
|---|---|---|
| Alarmed | Shaky | Timid |
| Scared | Startled | Restless |
| Panicked | Vulnerable | Uneasy |
| Threatened | Cautious | Doubtful |
| Shocked | Nervous | Concerned |
| Agitated | Tense | |
| Unsafe | Anxious | |
| Fearful | | |
| Frightened | | |
| Terrified | | |

# Life Is Hard, and Other Erroneous Misconceptions

## FAST FACTS
▼▲▼▲▼

Our beliefs govern our thinking.

Our beliefs are generally shaped in childhood.

We're not always aware of our beliefs.

All beliefs have pros and cons.

We have the power to change our beliefs.

## MONIE'S STORY

*You know, I was really kinda surprised when my doctor told me I was depressed. I mean, I'm still trippin' 'cause I've read magazine articles and seen stuff on television about it, but I didn't think any of that stuff fit me. When I saw that show "20/20," Barbara Walters was talkin' about women who cried all the time, couldn't sleep, and lost weight 'cause they felt too bad to eat. Honey, I'm just the opposite of all that stuff. It's been so long since I cried until I doubt that I still know how to do it, I can't get enough sleep, and I eat everything that ain't nailed down. I know I'm moody but I just figured it was because life's so damn hard most days. I'm twenty-five years old, Black, got two kids under the age of five years old, and I'm on welfare. I grew up hearing that if you made your bed hard you had to lay in it, so here I am. It's true I'm not happy with my life and all, but you know the old sayin', Mama said there'd be days like this . . . she just didn't say there would be so many of them.*

## WANDA'S STORY

*The other day out of the clear blue sky my sister Joyce asked me if I was happy. I've never thought much about being happy one way or another. I don't think much about how I'm feeling—what's the use? I mean most days I don't think too much about anything. I just do what has to be done and go on about my business. I guess if I stopped to really think about how I was feeling I would've had to say no, no I'm not happy, but I'm not unhappy either; I just take things as they come. It doesn't really do much good to complain, it's not like anybody can make it better. Everybody knows that life is hard; you get what you can, when you can, and while you can and keep on pushin'. I look at the news and think, what's the use of putting yourself out, for what? Folks are still homeless, hurtin' and killin' one another, kids dropin' out of school, men beatin' up women, women leavin' their babies in the trash, it's the same old thing day in and day out. We don't even know how to treat each other, yet we're the first ones to holler when something goes wrong. I feel so discouraged when I think about all the good work folks like Dr. King and John Kennedy did to make*

*our world a better place, and we're still in the same old shape.
I guess the most I can ever hope for is to just get from day one
to day two without hurting anybody. I may be happy one day,
but I don't count on it being one day too soon. Maybe when
we as a people get our act together and start doing right by
each other I'll feel better, but for right now I'll just deal with
things the best way I know how.*

## MARYROSE'S STORY

*My sister says I was born with "much attitude" and my
mother calls me her evil chocolate child, but the truth of the
matter is, I just don't believe in takin' a lot of stuff off of nobody. The world's a cold hard place and I ain't afraid to do
battle with it. I speak my mind 'cause I learned early on if I
didn't folks will run over you and I don't plan on being nobody's doormat if you know what I mean. I don't always like
having to be so hard about things but you just don't know
who you can trust. I trust myself and that's about it. I'm
thirty-three years old and I've seen a lot of casualties in my
time. I've been on my own since I was eighteen and I've
made my way by hook or crook and I've lived to tell about it
'cause I didn't let nobody, white or Black, large or small,
woman or man make a fool out of me. I watch my girlfriends
gettin' beat up by their so-called boyfriends, boo hooin'
cause their man is runnin' round on them and doin' all kinds
of crazy-ass shit, and I don't feel sorry for them, 'cause they
ask for it, being all sweetness and light. Not me, no ma'am
not me, not the kid; I'd kick their sorry asses to the curb and
keep right on steppin'. It's like if you're going to be with me,
you better come correct, or not at all. Linda, my sister, is always sayin' that I'm never goin' have a man, cause I don't
know how to be a little softer in my ways, but she can't talk
'cause her old man left her high and dry for some young
thang half her age last year. So she can't tell me diddly
about bein' with some man. I may not have a man now, but
when I do you can bet your bottom dollar I'm not goin' to let
him walk all over me, that's for damn sure.*

> "There's no normal life, Wyatt, there's just life,
> now get on with it."
> —Doc Holliday in *Tombstone*

Whenever I find myself suffering from a "stop the world I want to get off " kind of day, I head for my video collection and pop in one of my favorite tapes. My mood and circumstances generally dictate what I watch, and the other day was without a doubt the shoot-'em-up, ride-'em-out western kind. I was stressing hard. My son, who recently decided to move to California, was having a tough time finding a suitable apartment; my hair was in urgent need of perm repair and my hairstylist had the nerve to be on vacation; and to top it all off my beloved pooch, Boogie, who considers any command from me as optional, broke free of the backyard and headed for territory unknown, leading me on a merry chase all over the neighborhood. I was fit to be tied, my thoughts went into the automatic shift mode of life sucks, and my already down mood took a real emotional nosedive. Feeling worn out and physically spent, I did what I've done many times in the past: I tossed a video in the player, grabbed my pint of butter pecan crunch ice cream, turned on the set, and settled in to nurse my wounds, blaming myself and life for my woes. It was toward the end of the movie when Doc was dying and I was slowly fading in a butter pecan haze that Doc's one-sentence commentary on life, in his lazy raspy southern drawl, caught my attention.

*Pardon me for interrupting, sweetcakes, but as much as I can appreciate your fondness for westerns, and sympathize with your worries about your son and dog, is this story leading anyplace special?*

*—Zoey*

Sorry, I got carried away. The point I want to make is that I did what many of us do when we're emotionally overwhelmed and physically stressed—I fell into the clichéd belief trap. The minute I started the blame game I was ready to surrender my personal power to the belief that everything in my life was a failure. When I thought I was a failure, that was reflected in my mood. I began to notice that my thinking was directly related to how I was feeling and behaving. I think that so often we get caught up in the situations we're in at the moment that we lose our ability to give the situation an objective viewpoint.

*I hear what you're sayin', but to be real honest, half the time I'm not even sure I'm thinkin' when I'm stressed out. Most of the time it's like, okay this needs to be done or that has to be takin' care of . . . the next thing I know I'm worn down to the bone.*

*—Joyce*

*Girl, I heard that. Some days it's all I can do to remember my name, much less think about what I'm thinkin' about. I mean working sometimes ten- and twelve-hour days then having to come home and deal with the house and kids, at the end of the day I just want to fall into the bed and not think at all.*

*—Lyndey*

I can really appreciate what you're saying because it is hard to pay attention to what we think on a minute-by-minute basis. Let's face it, realistically we don't go around thinking about our thoughts, however we do pay attention to our mood. We notice when we're irritable, feeling down and tired. Our mood is often directly linked to what we're thinking and for the most part our thinking is related to whatever situation we're in at the moment. I was bummed out because I was thinking about the situation with my son, my hair, and my dog. I thought I was supposed to know what to do and when I discovered that I couldn't fix any of them, I started blaming myself and my life. When I was able to take a step back from the situations at hand I discovered that I didn't have to fix anything, actually all I had to do was take a reality check; my son wasn't going to be homeless, he was a grown man and very resourceful; I could always do my own hair, maybe not as well as my stylist but I did know how to use a comb and brush; and Boogie would come home when he felt like it as he always had in the past.

In the beginning I had, like many of us, believed that my low mood was generated by the situation that I found myself in at the time, and therefore my only option was to ride it out until its bitter end. But what I discovered was that my negative thoughts about the situation triggered my low, depressed mood and if I would give myself a chance to think about the situation I might feel differently.

*Well, I can see the connection, negative thoughts equal stressed-out feelings, but to be real honest it just seems so phony to think that we're going to go around havin' all these positive thoughts and feeling good all the time, especially when we're stressin' about something. My life just doesn't work that way, never has and probably never will. Seems to me if my thoughts were so negative I'd be worse off than I am now.*

*—Ella*

I agree with you, Ella, it would be phony to always have positive thoughts and feel good about everything all the time. But I learned that it's not always about thinking positive or feeling good, it's more about knowing that we have a range of options in how we see and feel about a situation. Most of the time when we're in a tough spot we don't recognize that there may be more than one way to view a situation. I discovered that there are some thoughts and feelings that are just middle of the road. I think a lot of the time we lock ourselves into believing that we only have one or two choices about things, including how we feel—something is either good or it's bad or there's a right way or wrong way to do something. That kind of thinking can create its own form of stress. When we feel boxed in from dealing with this type of stress it shows up in our mood. When our mood is low it triggers more negative thoughts and the depressed cycle begins.

*I'd like to say something here if I could. I know what you're talking about, sis, because we covered a lot of this kind of stuff in my rehab program. What we learned is that when we got stressed out it was more likely that we would start using again, so they taught us that we had to check in with our-*

*selves at different times during the day in order to stay on top of what we were feeling. It's like I know I'm having negative thoughts whenever I find myself in a situation that makes me say things to myself like "What's the use" or "Nobody understands me" 'cause that's what I used to tell myself just before I would start drinkin'. And whenever I'd tell myself those two things it was like I'd just given up on everything. I really have to watch myself when I go to bars and parties because those are really stressful situations for me. When I first got clean I couldn't go near them. Nowadays I steer clear of the bar scene pretty much, but I'll go to parties, and I have to really check in with myself in order to make sure I stay on track. I find that by asking myself three simple questions—I call it my two minute check-in—I'm able to stay on target.*

*—Cassie*

I use that method, too, Cassie, just asking myself three simple questions three or four times a day—and sometimes more if things get really hectic. It's simple. I can do it on the spot, and it works because it really helps in allowing me to monitor my mood and my thoughts.

*So tell me this, how does asking yourself a bunch of questions make you feel any better?*

*—Lyndey*

Asking yourself the questions doesn't necessarily make you feel better, but it does help you to check in with your thoughts and feelings before you get to that overwhelmed stressed-out mood. Try it for yourself and see what you notice.

What do I notice that's different about my situation
   right now?
On a scale of 1–10, would I rate my mood 1–3
   (low/undepressed) 4–6 (so, so) 7–9 (depressed)?
Can I do something differently? Yes/No

The first question helps us to assess the situation, the second question helps us to assess our mood in the situation, and the third question gives us the option of making a change for ourselves.

*I don't know, this seems pretty easy, and both you and Cassie say it helps you feel better. So if I do these questions I won't get depressed?*

*—Eboni*

It's not that you won't be depressed, Eboni, it's just that you'll have taken a step in checking your stress level and evaluating your thoughts about your situation. Our depressed mood feeds off stress and negative thinking. If we can decrease our stress level and adjust our thinking, then we have a good chance of decreasing depression.

*Well, I'm not sure I understand how knowing what I'm thinking is gonna make a difference in how I'm feeling.*

*—Queenie*

Actually, Queenie, it is more than just our thoughts that determine how we feel, our thoughts and mood are also governed by our personal belief system.

*I'm a little confused here, help me out, sis, what's the difference between what we think and what we believe? I've always considered them to be one and the same.*

*—Lyndey*

I tend to think of beliefs as our very own personal operator's manual for life. It's the system by which we choose to govern ourselves and the things we do on a day-to-day basis. Everybody has beliefs; some people call them values, some folks like my grandmother, Mama, call them common sense. For example: An act of kindness is its own reward, or Proper ladies never get angry, or—one of my personal childhood favorites—God don't like ugly, which generally referred to misbehavior, although the manner in which it was often used was open to question. Normally our beliefs are very private, tucked away inside our heads. We don't really think about what we believe or don't believe in our day-to-day lives—however there are a few values that have taken on universal appeal and as such have become national clichés, like the bumper sticker I saw the other day that stated ONLY THE STRONG SURVIVE—until we encounter a situation that challenges what we believe to be real or true.

Many of us use our beliefs to build life foundations for ourselves and our families, and these beliefs give us a means of coping with stressful situations. However, and this is the tricky part, very often the things we believe tend to be more hurtful than helpful. For example, if I believe that I'm a strong Black woman and as such, I should always be available to help my child, have my hair done just so and control my dog, and the situation arises where I can't do any of these I'm going to think that I'm a failure, because my thinking is locked into a belief system that dictates that I'm strong and I should be able to handle these situations. When our personal belief systems tend to be rigid it's reflected in our thinking; when our thinking is rigid it shows up in our mood. When I could allow myself to step back from my belief about being strong and needing to have a solution for everything I could see that I wasn't a failure. In reality these three incidents didn't represent my whole life, and my mood went from being low to being more so-so, which was not necessarily great but it was better. Our belief system is generally where we go to find comfort and peace, we look to our beliefs in order to find a means of coping, but what often happens is we find more confusion than comfort in the beliefs that we've designed for ourselves.

*I think I know the answer to this, but Lord help me, I'm gonna ask it anyway. Where in the world do all these beliefs come from?*

—Lyndey

*Wait, sis, let me tell her. From our parents, teachers, and everybody else along the way. Honey, I know if my mama hada had any idea of what she was doin' when she had me she woulda donated my egg to the Easter Bunny.*

—Eboni

*Eboni, girl, you know you ain't right. You need to quit.*

—Joyce

But Eboni *is* right, Joyce, we get a lot of our beliefs about ourselves and the world around us from our family members; after all, they are our first contact with the world. Our parents and family members weren't trying to hurt us, they passed on to us what had worked for them in their lives. My father's message to me that I could do anything I put my mind to was the same belief that helped him to establish his career as the first Black software engineer in a Fortune 500 company. And for the most part when I look at my father's life, and the belief system that helped him to make the accomplishments that he did, I have to say it worked for him. To some degree my father's belief also worked for me. However, as I started living my life I discovered that the obstacles I encountered were different, therefore I had to modify his belief so that it could be more flexible in order to work in my life. In all fairness, though, I must say that our families aren't the only ones who supply us with beliefs about the world. All we have to do is look at the media, television, newspapers, magazines, they all feed into our belief systems too. In the past week I've gotten four magazines that have told me in order to look and feel my best I need to wear a certain designer label, buy a special brand of makeup and lose x amount of weight. The message (belief) is that in order to look like the air-brushed model I have to believe I'm not okay as I am. And let's face it, these products wouldn't sell unless we believed what they're telling us.

*I believe I'm a good Christian woman, and that belief is all I need to get by. Maybe if more of us believed in the Word we wouldn't have to suffer such trials and tribulations. Maybe this depression you keep talkin' about is just a wake-up call, a crisis of faith.*

*—Queenie*

*I consider myself a good Christian too, Queenie. I still attend the church I grew up in and I try to live by the Word, and you know I believe in the power of prayer, but it's like not even that helps when I get in my low moods. Maybe this is what God intended my life to look like. It makes me feel worse to think I'm to be punished for something and I don't know what it is.*

*—Ella*

While I have a healthy respect for and very strong belief in the spiritual presence of a higher power, I also believe that our higher power doesn't punish or curse us with illness or any of the other questionable things that occur in our lives. However, I am willing to respect the fact that some folks do hold that belief, and all I can say is that if we believe that God gave us depression, then we need to look at the fact that She also gave us a means for dealing with the depression. God doesn't lock us into our belief system, we lock ourselves in. If the belief is that God is all good and all powerful and can make us whole through prayer, what happens when we pray yet continue to suffer from depression? Do we blame God? No, we blame ourselves, which I don't personally believe is or has ever been God's intent. The God I believe in, know, and respect is not a God of revenge. Mama always taught me that through God, you shall find a way, and I strongly believe that God has given us a way to help us combat depression. I think that it's great to have a strong belief in God and prayer; however, we want our belief to bring us comfort so we have to be flexible in how we form the beliefs that we choose to guide our lives. Our belief systems are amazingly powerful in that they shape our personal and global vision on a day-by-day basis, and in a way, our beliefs have an uncanny ability to prove themselves to be true.

*So what you're saying is that beliefs are kinda like magic. In other words if we believe in somethin' it'll happen.*

—Ella

*Girl, I know that can't be right 'cause I believe I should've won that Lotto Saturday night, and unless you know somethin' I don't, that two mil ain't cross my palm yet. 'Cause I truly believe I deserve to be rich.*

—Flo

Our beliefs aren't magic, Ella, but they can have a self-fulfilling prophecy effect. When we only expect bad things to happen to us, then that's all we focus on or recognize in our lives. For example: If you believe that you're being punished by God, you're going to look for evidence (things happening in your life) to support that belief. Even when something goes right or good in your life, you'll look for reasons to doubt or mistrust those things because your belief won't support those things.

*That still doesn't address my belief about winnin' the Lotto.*
*—Flo*

*Sweetcakes, you need to believe in gettin' about two or three more jobs and leave that Lotto alone, cause all it's doin' is takin' your hard-earned money.*
*—Zoey*

I'm with Zoey on that one, Flo, but if you have a deep belief in your ability to earn a million dollars then nothing will stand in your way. You just have to ask yourself *what am I willing to do differently?*

*You know, that kinda makes sense to me. When I think about it I remember when we were kids and we had a problem Mama would always say, "Well, you were smart enough to get yourself into it, now just sit your butt down and think your way out of it," and that's what we did. She'd make us sit in a chair in the kitchen until we could come up with some kind of solution for ourselves, and you know I still do that, but I never really thought about it until we started talkin'. So I guess you could say one of my beliefs is that I'm smart enough to think my way out of anything. I don't let too much of anything get in my way for too long.*
*—Joyce*

*I'm not sure what I believe or don't believe anymore. If something feels right today, it feels wrong tomorrow. I mean, I still believe I'm a good person and all that, but everything else is pretty much a toss-up. Like, I didn't believe I was depressed, but the more we talk, the more I think, well, maybe I am depressed. Lord, I sure don't like the sound of that, it makes me feel so weak, and I just don't want to believe that I'm a weak person.*
*—Ella*

I have an idea, Ella, if you're willing. Let's test out your belief about being weak. I'm going to ask you some questions and I want you to answer them honestly. What proof do you have that you're weak?

*I can't concentrate on anything.*

What other signs tell you that you're weak?

*I'm just in a funk all the time, I'm not happy.*

Have there been times recently, like in the past week, when you have been able to concentrate, and you haven't been in a funk?

*Well, let me see now, I went shopping with Joyce and that was okay, and I had to give a presentation at work on Tuesday, so I guess I was concentrating then.*

Did you feel weak at those times?

*No, but I wasn't really thinking about it then.*

When do you find yourself thinking about being weak?

*Mostly when something goes wrong at the office or at the end of the day when I'm tired and I start thinking about something I forgot to do at work.*

What do you tell yourself at those times?

*I never really paid attention, but I guess I say something like "I blew it," or "I really messed up."*

Do you blow or mess up something every day at the office?

*No, as a matter fact, my manager told me that my presentation was perfect, and she was proud of me. Okay, I get it, I see where you're going with this, you're trying to get me to see that I don't feel this way all the time.*

That's right. Even when we think we're feeling down all the time, we do have periods when our low mood shifts. The exercise we just did together is called "collecting evidence." We check in with ourselves to see if there's been a change in our mood. When we're feeling down it's hard to take in new information, because everything is filtered through our belief system, so if our beliefs are negative we need to give ourselves a way to check out the facts. Collecting evidence allows us to step back and look at the facts. We can even adjust our beliefs if we choose, in order to help us shift our mood.

*I guess it's like they say, sis. Nothing is carved in stone even when you believe that it is.*

—Zoey

That's right, Zoey, nothing is carved in stone, especially where our thoughts and beliefs are concerned. If the belief can stand up to the evidence test, then it's a good chance that the belief is worth keeping, but if you find that the evidence doesn't actually support the belief, then that would mean that it would be helpful to adjust the belief.

*I guess it bothers me to think that what I've been believing might be bad or wrong. I mean, I was always taught to believe in myself. Now what I hear you sayin' is that belief isn't okay. That really is confusing. Now what am I supposed to believe about myself? Am I a good person or a bad person?*
*—Ella*

You're a good person, Ella, and I'm certain that there's a lot of evidence to support that. However, it's important to remember that when we work on collecting evidence to support our beliefs we need to look at specific situations, one at a time. For example: My friend Gloria Jean was feeling really down for weeks about her sixteen-year-old son dropping out of high school, and his continued behavior of running around with a questionable group of friends. Now, Gloria Jean is a single parent, who's worked her way up the ladder and holds a position of authority in city administration. Randy, the youngest of four, has always been a very bright child who loves adventure and, as Gloria Jean says, he's got a mind of his own. Gloria Jean revealed to me that she felt like a failure and a bad mother because Randy dropped out of school. When I asked Gloria Jean what made her believe that she was a failure as a parent, she replied that those kinds of things didn't happen to good parents. I then asked her what types of things she believed that good parents do for their children. She stated:

"Well, they love their kids and keep them clothed and fed, send them to good schools, help them with their homework, get them involved in community programs, and keep them involved with the church."

I then asked if she'd done those types of things with Randy, and she replied yes, she had, she had done those things for all of her children because her family was the most important thing in her life. When I asked about her other three children, Gloria Jean responded with a note of pride:

"Well Bobby and Ronny, my twenty-one-year-old twins, will be graduating from college in June, and Denise, my eighteen-year-old daughter, is looking forward to starting a nursing school program at the community college in the fall. I guess I did all the right things with those three. I raised Randy the same way that I raised the others. I just don't understand what went wrong. I've always believed that I was being a good mother, I mean, I did the best I knew how and the three oldest turned out okay, but Randy, he's just always been a child that's had a mind of his own."

I asked Gloria Jean to consider the fact that she had raised all of her children the same way, and knowing that she did the best that she could, could it be possible that she was a good parent?

"Well, I know I love my kids, I just wish Randy wasn't so headstrong. He's not a bad kid, in fact he's smart as a whip. But I can't say I love him any less than the others. I just get so frustrated with him, I really worry about him."

I believed that Gloria Jean was a good mother, but she needed to believe it too, and that meant that she would have to be willing to adjust her belief system to include all the facts as opposed to looking at just one questionable incident in her life. So I asked her if she would be willing to consider all the facts, including how well her other children were doing, and how much she loved and cared for Randy as well, and see if that made a difference in her belief about herself as a parent.

"Well, like I said, I love all my kids. I did the best I could. Sometimes I wish I could have done more, but all in all for the most part, I can say I certainly believe I tried to be a good parent, and for the most part I have been a good parent."

Like Gloria Jean, many of us get caught in what I call the black and white zone. That's where we get stuck in believing something is either all black or all white, when in reality a lot of things in our lives fall into gray areas, and even those gray areas come in different shades. Collecting evidence or looking at the facts helps us to examine the different shades of gray. When Gloria Jean was able to take a clear look at the evidence of her parenting skills, she could see that she was doing all the things that, according to her, made her a good parent. Randy's behavior wasn't a reflection of her parenting skills, it was more a reflection of Randy's headstrong behavior.

*How do we know when our belief isn't working? I mean, if it's always worked before, how will we know when it needs to be adjusted?*

Most of the time it's difficult to challenge our beliefs when we're in the middle of a stressful situation. However, if we can give ourselves a chance to step back from the "eye of the storm," it might be a couple of hours or a couple of days, we can ask ourselves a few questions that might help us to get a clear thought as to whether or not we need to reevaluate our belief. Here's a little shortcut I use whenever I find myself in an emotional crunch and I need to step back from the situation. I ask myself the following five questions:

Why do I believe this is true?
How does this belief serve me at this time?
Do I have all the facts (evidence)?
Is there another way of viewing this situation?
Will my view of this situation change in twenty-four
    hours?

When I was a young girl, running around frettin' about one thing or another that I thought was going wrong in my life, Mama, my grandmother, would give me one of her exasperated looks and say in a quiet, chilling voice, "*Looka here lil' girl, life don't owe you no favors. You get out just what you put in, so if you think you want somethin' good to come outta that bucket, you better put somethin' in it and quit complainin'.* When I was younger, I would discount Mama's words in the belief that a) all grandmothers talked that way and b) her words didn't apply to me. As I've grown to adulthood, I've discovered that my grandmother's words held a lot of wisdom. Life didn't owe me anything, and if I wanted some good to come out of it then I had better look at what I was putting into my life. Being able to have some flexibility in regard to my belief system allows me to see shades of gray, instead of locking myself into the black and white zones of powerlessness. Life isn't "hard," it's just a bucket that we have to put something into in order to pull something out of it. Now, as Doc Holliday would say, "*Just get on with it.*"

# Belief Assessment

Everyone has beliefs, they're the backbone of our personal value systems, and include all those things that we hold near and dear to our hearts, such as our faith in God, the goodness of man- and womankind, and our belief in those that we love and care about in our lives. Many of our beliefs are shaped by our personal experiences, and our perceptions of the world in which we live. Our beliefs help us to look at ourselves and the world in a certain way, and serve as our personal support system. What we don't often recognize is the fact that sometimes our personal beliefs get in the way of our ability to feel good about ourselves and what we've accomplished, and these same beliefs can even get in the way of our willingness to accept others. The beliefs that get in our way have a name—they're called negative assumptions. Negative assumptions are generally recognizable in that they tend to make us feel upset, angry, and down on ourselves. The good news is that we have the power to change our beliefs, or at least assess the worth of what we're willing to believe. This exercise will help us to determine whether our beliefs are helpful or harmful.

## Belief Assessment

My belief is: _____

This belief serves me in these three ways:

    1. _____
    2. _____
    3. _____

This same belief is harmful to me in these three ways:

    1. _____
    2. _____
    3. _____

In order to have this belief serve me better I would like to revise it. My revised belief is:

_____

## Saying It Loud (Self-talk)

We all talk to ourselves, silently in our heads or mumbling half out loud as we go about our daily task. Most of the time these conversations are purely random, happening with little thought or acknowledgment, and at other times we're processing important information. We don't always recognize it, but these personal one-on-one conversations that we engage in are very important, and they can be very productive in helping us to validate our self-worth and move us out of a depressed state of mind. We've talked about how we give ourselves negative messages and how those messages can and often do bring us down. Well, this exercise will provide us the opportunity to give ourselves positive messages in the form of personal affirmations. Personal affirmations are a form of self-talk that work in the same manner as silent prayers. Saying them helps us to build inner strength. Affirmations also serve two other functions: Each time we give ourselves personal affirmations we block negative messages, and the more we say them the greater possibility we have of turning the affirmation into a positive personal belief. In order to be effective personal affirmations need to have three elements: they should begin with "I"—after all they belong to you; they need to be short; and they need to be direct. For example:

I have all the time I need.
I am a Black woman with dignity.
I am worthy of all that is good.

Create five personal affirmations. Write them down on notecards or post-its and keep them with you at all times so that you can refer to them often throughout the day. Notice how you feel before, during, and after saying your affirmation.

# Beatin' the Devil out of Depression

## FAST FACTS

Depression affects the way we think, feel, and act.

Depression is more than sadness or the blues.

Depression is known clinically as a mood disorder.

Depression is treatable.

## LASHAWN'S STORY

*I was diagnosed HIV positive four years ago, and I'd be lying if I said I wasn't really depressed in the beginning. I mean, I was like everybody else, saying it can't happen to me—well, it did, and let me tell you, honey, it rocked my world up and down and side to side. I blamed myself 'cause who else was there to blame? I was the one having unsafe sex, trying to be a party girl. I wanted to be popular and I was, but I never dreamed it could end up like this. I still get down on myself from time to time, especially when I think, "I'm only thirty years old and I'll never have kids," that's the part that hurts the most. I've been going to support groups at the women's clinic and that helps a lot, but in the beginning I have to admit I thought seriously about ending it all. I wrote my family and told them that I had a rare form of cancer, and I felt so bad, 'cause my mother, my aunt, and even my cousins flew out here to be with me. Seeing all of them made me feel worse 'cause I knew I was lyin' but I was too ashamed to tell 'em the truth. When they came to visit I closed myself up in my room and didn't come out for just about the whole two weeks they were here. All I could do was stay in the bed and cry. I didn't know what was worse: the HIV or the depression I was in when I thought about my family. When I didn't show up for my doctor's visit they sent a visiting nurse out to see me and that's when I told Mama and them the truth. My aunt Vernetta, Mama's younger sister, said she wanted to beat the livin' stuffin' outta me, but get this, it wasn't because of the HIV, but for lyin' to them. She was like, "Girl, don't you know we could've been working with you." Mama was hurt, I could tell, but she was like, "It's all water under the bridge now, tell us how we can help you." I swear to you, that's when I started feelin' better and I joined a support group. I still have the HIV, I'm always gonna have that, but the depression is gone, for now anyway. The love of my family means the world to me, and just knowing that I haven't lost them, well, now I feel like I can make it through anything.*

Child! If you don't leave me alone, I'm gonna
beat the devil outta you.

—Momi

This was Momi's favorite warning whenever we were close, but not quite there yet, to getting on what she called her last good nerve. Of course she never followed through with her dire warning, but it was a serious heads-up signal for us kids that something (generally our behavior) had better change . . . and fast. I can remember once asking Momi, in one of my gutsier childhood moments, how she would know that she had beat the devil out of us, and without skipping a heartbeat she laughingly replied,

" *'Cause when I'm through wearin' your lil' butt out, you'll behave like you have some sense."*

*"But, Momi, how do you know we have the devil in us?"* I asked, searching for clues.

*"Everybody has a lil' devil in 'em, baby, and you know when it's there 'cause it makes you act up,"* she told me as she headed to the kitchen to start dinner. *"But you know what,"* she said, smiling and looking back over her shoulder, *"you can't beat the devil you don't know, always remember that."*

You can't beat the devil you don't know. My mother's words softly vibrated in my ears as I sat looking out of my bedroom window. I missed her terribly. How many days have to go by before you stop counting? Evenings and Sunday afternoons are still the hardest. Those were the times when she and I would talk for hours, burning up the phone lines giggling like schoolgirls over silly trivia; sharing gossipy tidbits we'd read about our favorite movie stars in *People* magazine; bragging about the great finds we'd made at bargain basement closeout, liquidation, and last-chance-to-shop sales; and just plain old talking about everyday woman stuff. After long hard years of adolescent struggle, and my immaturity as a young woman, Momi and I had become friends. She was my mother: *"Girl, I know that's not makeup I see on your lil' fresh face";* my mentor: *"No, baby, let me show you how to cut up a chicken";* my girlfriend:

*"Girl, let me tell you what I found at this garage sale,"* and my anchor: *"Don't worry, baby, you're gonna do just fine."*

As I moved through life, inching my way toward maturity, Momi was always there to encourage me to beat the devil I didn't know. It was Momi who lent a steady hand as I began discovering and dealing with my inner devil on an adult level. It was she who allowed me to unravel the painful thoughts that held me hostage in a state of emotional unrest. And it was her soothing voice that encouraged me to take another step when all I wanted to do was lie down and give up the fight. I knew I could count on Momi, even when I sometimes didn't want to, and then . . . she died. When I learned of her death, I screamed at God, and cried myself into a physical clasp of numbness. I waited for the world to stop, and when it refused to comply I mentally took on the task myself. Strangely enough, I wasn't afraid of the devil that claimed me, I knew it's name . . . depression. I was familiar with the threatening signs: the empty void of emotional detachment; the fact that I had none of the energy required to experience feelings; the depth of the raw sorrow that sucked the life from my body leaving me vacant, a hollow shell. Momi, the woman who had blessed me with life, had drawn her last breath, leaving me alive to struggle with the devil on my own.

Everyone, in their own well-meaning, helpless fashion—family members, doctors, therapist, and friends—tried to reassure me that my feelings, or lack thereof, were a normal part of the grief process.

Give yourself time, baby, maybe you can find some comfort in knowing that she's out of pain.

Try not to be so sad, she's not really gone, she'll always be with you.

I'm so sorry for your loss, and I know your pain is deep, just remember you can survive this and we'll help all we can.

Heartfelt words, words expressing sorrow, words meant to comfort and words of encouragement, mountains of words and I heard them all, but I couldn't take them in. Emotional numbness doesn't allow words to make sense. I didn't feel sad, that would have required energy. I didn't need time, time was a quiet opportunist stealing minutes and hours, leaving weeks in their place. And surviving wasn't an option I could take or leave, survival was the automatic door that I stumbled through with the words . . . she's gone. I needed the comfort that only Momi knew how to give, I needed her words to help me beat the devil out of the hurt, numbness, and pain that threatened to eat me alive, and she took those words with her.

As the weeks slipped into months, I found myself mentally counting off each day: three days since she's been gone, five days since she's been gone, twenty days since . . . it became a game, like the one Momi had taught me to play as a little girl whenever she was going to be out of my sight for periods of time. *"Here, baby, count on your fingers like this, and before you get to the lil' finger on your other hand, Momi'll be right back."* And she'd disappear into another room, only to return as promised before I'd get to the little finger on my other hand. Unbeknownst to Momi, that little game had become one of my main survival tools for beating the devil, substituting minutes, hours, and days for fingers as I got older, but always knowing that wherever I was all I had to do was pick up the phone, and *"Momi'll be right back."* But not this time, this time Momi couldn't keep her promise, but I didn't know what else to do, so I just kept counting and waiting, picking up the phone at odd hours and punching in the familiar digits, only to hang up on the first ring.

Everyone thought I was grieving, I had them all fooled. I knew what grief looked like. Honest grief had a clear beginning, a middle, and ending. It had been six months and I had made the discovery that counting never had to end. Numbers can go on forever. I knew this because I was still counting, one hundred eighty days since she's . . . My sadness slipped effortlessly into the seductive haze of depression without fanfare while I busied myself ticking off the numbers, two hundred days since . . . Like a long lost friend that drops in from time to time I recognized signs of the depression's presence, and being a good hostess, I made room for its extended stay in my life. My daily routine of going to work and coming home took effort but wasn't impossible; I had mastered the art of being physically present a long time ago. I didn't interact with friends or participate in activities as much as I usually did, but after all I wasn't expected to, people thought I was grieving. When they did question my absence from their lives I politely told them a necessary lie, *"I'm working on a project right now,"* or *"I'm in the process of writing a new book and it's really taking up all of my time."*

I lied to everyone else but I couldn't lie to myself. The depression was starting to get in my way, it was becoming less of a welcome visitor and more of a worrisome intruder, making me irritable, disrupting my concentration, and demanding more and more of my energy. The devil was starting to beat me, and I was scared.

*"Lynda, I need an appointment to see you. It's back and I can't write."*

I'd never been this afraid before, writing had always been my salvation. Writing was the one friend that I could count on, mainly because it failed to be intimidated by the emotional bully that often held me captive. In the past I always knew that I could put pen to paper and push the numbness aside. Writing gave me the room I needed to breathe. But not this time. My depression was becoming more demanding, it was taking my attention from the one thing that I was unwilling to give up . . . my creative voice.

"When is it going to stop? I can't keep on like this, I just can't." I sobbed into my hands.

"How long have you felt this way?"

"Too long, it used to come and go before, but now it's ruling my life. I can't think, I can't write, and I'm just worn out. You've got to help me," I heard myself beg.

"Are you suicidal?"

"Well, I wouldn't try to hurt myself, but if a bus was coming while I was crossing the street I don't know that I'd jump out of the way."

"I know you've managed to move through these depressed times before, but this time it's really wearing you down. Maybe we need to consider a more aggressive approach."

"What does that mean?"

"I was thinking about the use of medication."

"Is that the only answer?" I asked timidly.

"No, it's one of the options," she replied calmly.

As my doctor went on to explain the various kinds of anti-depressants and their function in relieving the symptoms of depression, I found my mind wandering into the familiar territory of doubt. "And Prozac is another . . ." Snatches of my doctor's one-sided conversation floated in and out of my daydream like a haze as I thought about the controversy, criticism, and heated debate that surrounded the uses of medication in the Black community.

*Girl, I don't even want to deal with nobody's drugs. My friend Cora is all strung out now 'cause she got some pills from a friend of hers that was supposed to help her lose weight. The only thing she's lost is her mind. I've been talkin' to her tryin' to get her to come see you, Cassie, down at the women's center, but she doesn't believe she has a problem. I feel so bad for her. First her brother got locked up, and then she lost her job, now she's all shacked up with some old joker that just uses her. Now there's a sistah that I would say is seriously depressed. She's told me that she wants to stop usin' but every time I offer to help she just get's all freaked out. I really can't blame her, she's afraid that if she goes for help, she'll end up in jail. I keep trying to tell her that they won't lock her up for gettin' help, but if she keeps using, they're either goin' lock her butt up or she's goin' to kill her silly self.*

*—Ella*

*She sounds like she's got some serious stuff goin' on. If she's willin' to come down to the center I'll talk to her, Ella. If she's using that much, it might mean she's trying to self-medicate. We see that a lot at the center; sistahs come in to get clean, but a lot of them are afraid of getting off of the drugs and alcohol because they can't handle the feelings of depression or anxiety. Maybe I can get one of our doctors to assess her to see if she needs to be on meds.*

*—Cassie*

*Now does that make any kind of sense, they come into rehab to get clean, and you all put them right back on drugs. Sounds like that's defeating the mission, don't you think?*

*—Flo*

*I use anti-depressants, in fact, I'm not ashamed to admit it. They saved my life when I got off of drugs. And I know it sounds strange but takin' the medication helps me to stay clean.*

—Cassie

*Girl! Aren't you afraid of becoming addicted again? Who knows what those folks are really givin' you?*

—Queenie

*I'm not addicted to anti-depressants, I was addicted to alcohol and cocaine. Actually, my counselor said that I was probably trying to self-medicate my depression all along by using that stuff. I can tell you this much, I feel a whole lot better since I've been using the medication. I was scared to use it at first, 'cause I was afraid it would lead me back to the other stuff, but so far I'm takin' it one day at a time. You know, while I was in treatment we had to talk about our families and I figured out that I learned how to drink from my father. Daddy would come home at the end of each day and pour himself a scotch and water. I never saw his glass empty from the time he came home till we went to bed at night. He called his drink his friend, "I'm gonna take my friend and go read the paper," or "me and my friend are going to go pay the bills." Whenever he was dealing with something he would say "Me and my friend will figure it out." I grew up thinking that if alcohol could be Daddy's friend then it could be mine. I started using cocaine when I started running with my college roomie, but alcohol has always been my drug of choice. I didn't learn how to use drugs by having some doctor give them to me.*

—Cassie

*I know where Queenie's coming from. It's like, what kind of message are we giving to our younger brothers and sistahs out there if they see us puttin' drugs in our bodies? We're tellin' them one thing and doin' another. We can't tell them to solve their problems by runnin' to the doctor for pills.*

—Eboni

*Lord! Lord! What's it all comin' to, what happen to the good old days when we cured ourselves? I remember whenever we felt poorly, my mama, bless her heart, would go out in back of the house—we used to call it the woods—and pick herself a lil' of this and a lil' bit of that, come back, boil it all up in a tea, and give it to us to drink. Shoot, before you could say "jack rabbit" we were back feeling like our old self again. Mama use to call everything "the misery." "Come and drink some of this here tea for your misery," she'd say. 'Course that was years and years ago and we lived down South in the country, and we didn't have money for doctors and such in them days. Nowadays at the first sign of a sniffle folks go runnin' off to the doctor with their hands out for pills. I think that's what's wrong with some of us today. We depend too much on other folks to make us feel right with ourselves.*

—Queenie

*Shoot, Queenie, my mama used to do the same thing. I grew up in Mississippi and whenever we didn't feel good, she'd go dig up her roots and strip bark off of trees and cook it down, except Mama would always put a generous taste of corn liquor in the mix and call it her "remedy." If the remedy didn't cure your butt that dose of corn whiskey was enough to kill whatever ailed you; either way, you felt better in the end. I seriously believe Mama's remedies is the cause of my older brother Milton being an alcoholic to this day, 'cause he was always ailin' with one thing or another when we were growing up. But I've got to admit we didn't stay sick for long after she got finished dosing us up. And back then nobody ever heard of depression, cancer, or any of the other kinds of sickness we've got today. We've got to give it to the old folks, back then they got by on the church, and motherwit, pure and simple.*

—Flo

*I'm sittin' here listenin' to you all talk about the old days, but I don't remember them always bein' all that good. We had doctors, but we couldn't always afford to go to them, and a lot of that stuff our mamas cooked up didn't cure us. It might've made us feel better for a time, but that's about all.*

*As for myself, it wasn't so much what my mamma cooked up, it was the fact that I got a lil' personal attention from her and that's what made me feel better. But I also know that folks died back then too, they died from some of the same stuff that's killin' us now. It's like you said, Queenie, they called stuff "the misery," but half the time that misery was every- thing from monthly cramps to cancer. I think the only reason we didn't have pills to cure stuff is 'cause we couldn't get pills to cure it. Shoot! I ain't even gonna lie, I'll tear the door down gettin' to my doctor's office if I'm hurtin' bad enough, and if I'm givin' the younger brothers and sisters the wrong message by takin' medication, then maybe they'll follow me to the doctor's instead of gettin' what they think they need off of the street. Besides, it's about time we start making a difference between medication and street drugs 'cause we're grown enough to know the difference.*

—Zoey

*I think it's one thing to take pills when you're hurting physi- cally, but when you take drugs to control your mind that's something altogether different. I think if some doctor gave me pills for depression or something like that, I don't know if I could take them; I'd be afraid they'd do something to my mind like take away my control. Anyway, how do we know how all that stuff is affecting our bodies? I read this article in* Time *or* Newsweek, *I can't remember which one now, and it was talkin' about how all these people were having bad side effects from using stuff like Prozac, and all those other drugs out there. You know what they say, don't believe the hype; well, I'm a firm believer in not believing.*

—Ella

*I don't know about what happened with other people, all I can tell you is none of that stuff happened to me. In fact I didn't realize that I could live life without struggling inside so much until I started taking my medication. Personally I don't think the medication I use takes away my control, I think it gives me control. To be real honest, it never even dawned on me that I was depressed, I just thought, well maybe this is what my life's always going to look like. Then*

*when I started taking the medication I found that I felt better
and my life started lookin' better.*

*—Cassie*

*"So what do you think?"* My doctor's question snapped
me back to the present. *"Would you like to try a trial of anti-
depressants?"*

I wish I could say that I went away from that session
in calm resolve to do so, but that's not the case. It actually
took several sessions of talking and mentally struggling
with the idea of using medication to help me deal with my
depression.

When I thought about previous conversations with my
sister circle, and my own experience with feeling weighted
down by life's circumstances, I recognized that we could
call it whatever we wished: "the blues," "being in a funk,"
"the misery," "mood swings," and "beatin' the devil," the
name we gave it really didn't matter. When confronted with
the facts, the evidence always comes out the same . . . depression. I believe that as Black women we want to believe
that if we deny its (depression's) existence we can control
the outcome, but unfortunately depression thrives on denial, as it slowly moves into our lives claiming one necessary life function after another like a thief in the night. Like
the rest of the population that suffers from this disorder at
one time or another we find ourselves robbed of sleep, concentration, energy, pleasure, and creativity, in essence, all
of the things that give one a sense of purpose and enhances
the quality of human life. We remain wedded to our historic
belief of being strong Black women emotionally and physically, at all costs, and sometimes, especially where our
health is concerned, that cost is much too high. For many of
us, the thought of taking medication for something other
then a "bona fide" physical ailment seems repugnant. We
don't want a "superficial" remedy to have more control over
our life than we have. The reality is that when we're in a depressed state, we surrender to the will of the depression,
which gives us the illusion of being in control. As if our own
inner struggles with depression aren't enough, we find ourselves worrying about what friends, family, and colleagues
would say "if they knew" we not only weren't being "strong"

but to top it off that we had to "take something" in order to get back on track. When we can't even bring ourselves to say the word "depression," how are we going to explain it to a generation of Black folks whose ancestors survived the Middle Passage in chains?

As for myself, I felt in my heart of hearts that I could handle whatever questions, concerns, and suspicions others might have about the validity of my taking medication; however, like many of my sisters I didn't know if I could tame my own demons in the arena of strong Black woman vs. anti-depressant medication. Now that I knew my devil by name, I was ready to give it a serious heads up, to fight back, as Malcolm X said, by any means necessary. The thought of taking medication scared me, but the depression scared me more. It was now my turn to beat the devil.

# A Body of Knowledge

FAST FACTS
▼▲▼▲▼

Depression slows down the mental and physical processes.

Physical activity helps to decrease depression.

Set small daily exercise goals.

## JOHNNI'S STORY

*I still can't believe this is happening to me, it's like a bad dream. I keep asking myself what did I do to deserve this, I mean, I'm a good person and all. I finally got my life on track and going the way I want it to go, with a good husband, good job, I just closed on the house of my dreams, and now I find out that I have breast cancer. I just can't believe it, why now, Lord? Why now? I'm not ready to have to deal with this. I'm forty-two years old and never been sick a day in my life. I've been to three doctors and they all say the same thing. I'm so numb till I can't even cry anymore. Art, my husband, just says that we'll take whatever steps we need to take, but this is my body we're talking about here. My body! Oh God! What am I going to do? The doctor says that it doesn't have to be a death sentence, but I've read the articles and there aren't any guarantees even when you catch it in time. Just when I have everything to live for, this happens. I don't smoke, I stopped drinking years ago, and I try to live a healthy life, why now? I've been in a fog all day. I can't even remember how I got home from my last doctor's appointment. I haven't told my family yet 'cause I can't deal with their pain and my pain too. One minute I'm mad at the world and the next minute I'm crying my heart out. It's like all this time I've been doing all the right stuff and for what, just so something like this could happen to me? I know this sounds crazy but the other night I got out of bed, it must have been about 3 o'clock in the morning, and got into a scalding hot shower and scrubbed until I was raw. I guess I thought I could scrub the cancer out of my body. Poor Art, I must have really scared him, 'cause he picked me up out of the shower and just wrapped his arms around me and we sat on the bathroom floor and cried together. The worst part of all this for me is thinking about him. I really love this man and I'm not ready to leave him yet. The one thing that keeps me going is knowing that I have him by my side. But Lord knows I'm just not ready for this now. I keep hoping every day that the doctors will call me and tell me that they've made a mistake. There's a part of me that knows that won't happen, but I can't help hoping.*

## DENISE'S STORY

*I know something's wrong with me and I think it might be cancer but the doctors tell me they can't find anything. They've run all kinds of tests and they still can't find nothing. My whole body hurts sometimes, and I keep getting these headaches. At first they thought they were migraines but my symptoms don't seem to fit. Most days I can get along okay, but last Tuesday I couldn't even get out of the bed. I had a low-grade fever, and the pains in my stomach were awful. When I went to my doctor she just shook her head and told me that she couldn't find anything wrong. I know my blood pressure's been a little high, but it shouldn't be causing me this kind of pain. I'm scared they're going to find something and it's going to be too late to do anything about it. I read in* Good Housekeeping *where this woman had this rare disease and she almost died before the doctors figured out what was wrong. My doctor keeps talking about stress, but I should know when I'm stressed, hell, raising five kids all by myself is bound to be stressful, but I shouldn't be hurting like this. I can tell you what's causing me stress, them not finding out what's wrong with me, that's what's causing me stress. I know my body and I know when something's wrong with me. I don't trust none of them if truth be told. They think that just 'cause I'm Black and don't have much money they can treat me any old kind of way and I'll accept it, but they're wrong. I'm going to keep going to the clinic and I don't care if I have to see every doctor in that place—somebody's going to figure out what's wrong with me. I watched my father die from heart complications and all those doctors could do was stand around and scratch their heads talkin' bout he waited too late to get help. My father was strong as an ox, he worked two jobs and he'd never been sick a day in his eighty-five years, and they were telling us he waited too late. Well I'm not waiting. I want answers, somebody somewhere knows what's wrong with me, and I'm not going to rest until they tell me what's going on with my body.*

When in doubt, work out.

—Personal credo

Anyone who knows me knows that I have a love affair with the gym. Earphones in place, water bottle at the ready, towel slung over my shoulder, and I'm prepared to take on the world . . . the world of Universal, Lifecycle, and Cybex workout machines. I move from machine to machine pacing myself each time, testing my stamina, woman against machine, or so I like to pretend. The machine usually wins, but that's not the point. The point is I'm working off my stress. I joined the gym in 1987 right after joining the Black Women's Health Movement and it's one of the smartest choices I've ever made in my life, for my life.

I'll never forget the first Black Women's National Health Conference I attended. I went from one workshop to another, absorbing bits and pieces of health-related educational information designed for me as a Black woman. There were workshops on relaxation, healthy eating habits, parenting, and relationships, but the one workshop that really captured my attention was on physical fitness. Wear comfortable clothing, the brochure advised, and be prepared to get busy. I had been meaning to get back into exercising for months and this workshop looked like it was going to give me the perfect opportunity to put my plan into action. *"What's the simplest thing you can do to save your life?"* the speaker asked in a booming voice, and after a timely pause, she gave the answer. *"Take a walk. Walk around the house, the yard, down the street, to the store, up or down stairs, walk the kids, the dog, I don't care where you do it, but do it. Do it three times a week, or better yet, do it every day for twenty minutes and I guarantee that the life you save will be your own."* She chanted in a singsong voice, pumping her legs up and down like a drum majorette waiting for the downbeat. *"Now come on, ladies, let's get those bodies moving"* and away we went moving from the courtyard onto the street, walking at a brisk pace as a united group, arms swinging back and forth, across the college campus. In the hour following our two-mile trek around the campus I learned that taking a walk increases energy and heart rate, and lowers blood pressure and stress. What can I say, that one walk led to another and the next thing I knew I was hooked. Within a month I became a full-time gym junkie. I discovered that working out not only helped to keep my body fit, it helped to keep my mind fit as well. I could work up a sweat and clear out the stress at the same time, and to top it off I felt good doing it.

*I started back joggin' last summer, and I have to admit I do feel better after a good run. I keep tellin' myself I'm workin' my way up to doin' the Labor Day ten-run but I'm in no big hurry.*
*—Joyce*

*Honey, the only way I'm gonna run anywhere is if somethin' awful big is gonna be chasin' me. I used to like goin' to the clubs and dancin' but that gets old after a while. Plus these bones aren't what they used to be. But don't get me wrong though, 'cause this old body can still shake a pretty mean tail feather.*
*—Flo*

*I like taking long walks, but the weather's been so crummy lately till I just don't like being out. Besides, I've already had a cold three times this year and going out in this weather just sets me up for getting it again.*
*—Ella*

Actually, Ella, I learned that taking a walk daily or doing any type of physical exercise might keep you from catching a cold. It's not the weather that makes us sick, it's our body's inability to handle stress that causes most of our health-related problems. With proper care our bodies are designed to handle any kind of change in the weather. When we get continuous colds or flu viruses it may be more than the weather that's making us sick.

*Last year when my friend Frankie had to be put in the hospital for a bleeding ulcer, she said the first thing her doctor told her was that she had to start seein' a counselor. I have to admit girlfriend has been goin' through a lot: she's raisin' those kids by herself, and she's been workin' two jobs just to make ends meet.*

*—Cassie*

Sometimes I think we neglect to recognize the power of stress on our bodies. At the conference I attended I learned that stress can mimic any physical illness from a cold to a heart attack. Ongoing stress can work to break down our immune system, which in turn makes us more vulnerable to illness and disease. I now think of my outbreaks of eczema as my body's way of telling me that I'm on stress overload.

*Sis, are you sayin' that when we're hurtin' that it's all in our heads? 'Cause if you are I feel a strong objection' comin' up. If there's one thing that I know real well, it's pain. Sometimes I get headaches so bad until I can't see straight and it just really ticks me off when I hear people talk that mess.*

*—Joyce*

I would never discount the reality of pain. I believe that pain is the body's way of signaling us that something is wrong, and we always need to pay serious attention to any type of pain we're having in any part of our body. I'm just saying that we need to also look at the fact that there may be more than one reason for the pain. I also believe—and I want you to hear me out on this—I believe that as Black women it's sometimes easier for us to recognize and accept help for our physical ailments than it is for us to deal with our emotional hurts. We talked about this before but it bears repeating: Emotional pain is just not acceptable in our community. Inability to cope with problems is seen as a weakness, and we brand ourselves as a failure for not being able to handle life. We view physical pain as being much more legitimate in terms of allowing ourselves to receive care, and even then we often wait until the pain is intolerable before we accept help. We need to recognize that we experience pain mentally and physically. It's our body telling us that it just can't take the emotional burden anymore, so it slows down in order to make us pay attention. This pain of depression is just as real as any other pain we experience, and we owe it to ourselves to treat it just as we would any other form of pain.

*All I know is that when I hurt, I hurt, and I want relief. I don't especially care where the pain is comin' from, I just want somebody to fix it, know what I mean? Every time I go into the E.R. the doctors treat me like I'm some kind of nut case or drug addict. I don't want to talk about what's goin' on at home and at work, I want something to take away the pain. Now my doctor is havin' me attend relaxation classes and a pain management class. I don't want to manage the pain, I want them to give me something to relieve the pain.*

*—Joyce*

I really understand your frustration, Joyce, and I don't blame you one bit for being so upset, but I also recognize that doctors aren't miracle workers. They can give us all the medicine in the world, but if the pain is triggered by something other than a physical cause the medicine will only offer temporary relief. I know it may not be what you want to hear, but maybe the doctor was trying to offer you some alternative for managing the triggers that cause the pain.

*I hear what you're sayin' and I'm willin' to give the classes a try, but all I know is when those headaches hit all I want is relief. You talk about stress causin' depression, but I get depressed when I'm hurtin', because I know that I'm gonna go through a hassle tryin' to deal with those doctors to get any kind of medication.*

*—Joyce*

Physical pain can cause us to be depressed, and I firmly believe in taking care of the physical pain first, but for long-term relief we have to start taking care of ourselves. We can't allow our beliefs about being emotionally strong to prevent us from seeking help, or rely on the doctor to always fix our physical pains when we're hurting. We've got to be willing to start doing some preventive self-care. Physical activity allows us to build physical as well as mental stamina. I've discovered that when I'm in shape it's easier to tackle the mental challenges that I encounter on a daily basis. I'm always amazed at how much we expect our minds and bodies to endure when it comes to the daily situations in life. We support families, work full-time jobs outside and inside our homes, have various social obligations, and we expect to be able to handle it all. For the most part we do, not recognizing that each of these commitments is producing levels of stress. Work stress, family stress, and social stress build up, and pretty soon it affects our energy reserves, and takes a large toll on our bodies. More and more sisters each year are dealing with illnesses like high blood pressure, migraine headaches, stomach ulcers, viral infections, eating disorders, and sleep disorders. When our bodies aren't working properly we worry and when we worry we get depressed.

*So you're sayin' we should get out and walk around the block or join a gym and we won't get sick or depressed, is that it? That doesn't sound like it would be much of a cure.*

*—Eboni*

*Listen up, sweetcakes, we don't have a cure for breast cancer, high blood pressure, or AIDS either, but there are preventive measures we can take, and if I'm hearin' right depression is in that same boat. Now I don't know about anybody else but if I'm willin' to rub my breast once a month, throw away salt, and use a condom to save my life, I can take on one more thing.*

*—Zoey*

I'm saying that there is cause and effect in terms of stress and illness. Our minds and bodies are one, when we take care of one we take care of the other. No, physical exercise won't stop us from getting ill, but it can serve as a preventive measure in helping us to lower our stress and building our physical and mental endurance. Physical exercise helps us to build and store the energy we need to cope with life situations.

*I understand all of that, but how does that help me when I'm hurtin'? I can tell you up front that the last thing I'm gonna do when my head starts hurtin' is think about this conversation. The truth of the matter is when my headaches start, thinkin' is the last thing I'm able to do.*

*—Joyce*

The next time you get a headache, check in with your doctor so that you can get something to relieve the pain. After the pain has stopped, get a pencil and paper and ask yourself the following questions.

What were your thoughts before the pain started?
What were you doing right before the pain started?
How intense was the pain on a scale of 1(low) to
    5(high)?
What did you notice that was different about the pain?

Keep a written log of your headaches for about a month and see if you notice any different or similar traits. By being able to track your headaches you'll have an idea of what some of your headache triggers are, and once you know the triggers you may be able to stop the headache before it starts or at the very least lower the intensity of the pain.

*You know, I really understand where Joyce is coming from because I have a hard time trusting doctors, especially after what happened to my grandmother. It seems like we had to fight every doctor at County Hospital just to get them to do anything for her when she had her heart attack. The doctors just wanted to talk about her age and the fact that a bypass might not help because her heart was too weak. M'dear, my grandmother was one of the strongest women in mind and body that I've ever known, and it just tears me up that it took those doctors so long to help her. She passed last spring, but I still believe that if those doctors had've acted sooner she'd still be here today. It wasn't somethin' in her head that was hurtin' her, it was her heart.*

*—Flo*

*I know just what you're sayin', Flo. You all might be too young to remember this, but I can still remember how in the forties and fifties down South when white folks wanted to get Blacks off the streets, they'd pick 'em up and throw 'em in the back wards of the county hospital where they kept all the crazy folks. Now I'm not sayin' that that kind of stuff goes on today, but you all got to admit sometimes things ain't always what they're cracked up to be with doctors and hospitals. You go in the door talkin' about your body hurtin' and they tell you it's all in your head.*

*—Queenie*

*I've heard those stories too, Queenie, and God knows you're telling the truth, but I've also got to believe that there are some righteous doctors out there somewhere. They can't all be bad, and I don't believe they are.*

*—Zoey*

*I guess I don't have a hard time dealing with the medical community, 'cause I work at the women's clinic, and plus goin' through rehab I've had the advantage of gettin' up close and personal with a few of the docs at the center. It's not that I trust all of them, mind you, but I don't think they're all out to get us. Look at Dr. Joycelyn Elders, that sistah's got it goin' on, and I just read an article in* Heart and Soul *magazine where she was talkin' about depression. Now she's a doctor that I'd trust in a heartbeat to take care of my mind and body.*

*—Cassie*

I've heard all of the medical horror stories too, and I can't blame folks for being skeptical at times, but when we get caught up in all the bad things that have happened, we lose sight of a lot of the good that happens. I agree with Zoey, there are some irresponsible professional folks out there, but I also know that there are some really caring professionals that we can trust. The more I work in the medical community the more I recognize that many of the physical problems we deal with are related to stress.

*I've been seeing Dr. Dickson for years and I think I trust her 'cause she's a sistah and she knows her stuff. So when she tells me something, I listen, and I don't have problems trusting her direction mainly because I've known her for a long time. If I was hurting I'd call her in a hot minute, but as much as I like and trust her I just can't see myself talking to her about all my personal problems.*

*—Lyndey*

*You know, for me it's not so much a matter of trusting doctors, hospitals, or anything else, it's more a matter of me feeling like I can trust myself enough to know when I can trust everybody else. I'll be real honest with you, I pay a lot of lip service to being a strong Black woman, but half the time I don't really know what that means. I'm physically in good health, I could stand to lose about five or ten pounds, but for the most part my last physical checkup was pretty good. It's like I'm hurting, but I'm not really in pain. I don't know, it's just that I don't always feel as solid as I'd like to feel. It's really hard to explain.*

*—Ella*

*Maybe it would help, Ella, if you went and talked to somebody, because the feelin' you're describing sounds a lot like the feelins I used to have when I was usin' alcohol and drugs. I knew deep down inside myself that I needed to stop using, but whenever I'd try to do it on my own the empty feelin' was just too strong and I couldn't cope, so I'd go back to using. My family kept waitin' and sayin' that I'd quit when I hit bottom, but what they didn't know was that I was already on the bottom emotionally and the drugs and alcohol kept me from stayin' there. When I was drunk or high I didn't have to worry about feelin' anything except high. I was afraid of what I felt: I was having feelin' for other women, and I was afraid of my family's disapproval. Not that they liked what I was doin' with the drugs or alcohol, but at least I didn't have to hide that from them. There was even a time when I thought seriously about killin' myself, and I think that's what got me into treatment. It wasn't easy opening up to a counselor, but I'm glad I took the risk to do it. Workin' at the women's clinic, it breaks my heart to see how some of those sistahs come in there, all broke down and hurtin'. It's like they've lost all hope. And I know nine times out of ten that they're lookin' that way because they're scared to tell anybody how much they're hurtin' on the inside. Pardon me for cryin' but I just get so worked up even talkin' about it.*

*—Cassie*

*You're okay, sweetcakes, we're with you, come 'n over here and let me massage your neck and shoulders. There are lots*

*of ways to deal with pain, Ella; it might not be a bad idea to
talk to a doctor, or a counselor.*

*—Zoey*

*It's not that I don't believe what you're sayin', Cassie, it's
just that you're talkin' about a pain that I don't feel, or
maybe I am feelin' it and just don't know it yet. I mean I'm
not hurtin' in that way, at least I don't think I am. I've never
thought about killing myself, and like I said, I have my down
days, but I always get through. To be honest I did think
about going to see a counselor, but then I thought, What
could she tell me that I didn't already know? I mean, if I was
physically hurting then it wouldn't be a problem for me to go
and see a doctor. I've read about depression, but everything
I've read sounds so, so—I don't know—some of it makes
sense, but it just doesn't seem to fit for me.*

*—Ella*

Zoey made an important point. There are a lot of ways to
deal with pain, but I'm aware that we may not recognize that
we're in pain, because depression doesn't always present itself as being physically painful. As Black women we've
grown up on the theory that many things in our lives are going to be difficult, and some of the things that we'll have to
endure will cause us physical pain, but we don't talk about
emotional pain. We describe our hurts in terms of our bodies
and we seek relief to ease those hurts, but I'm aware that it's
hard to describe a sense of pain that we've never learned to
recognize. The first time I experienced depression I didn't
recognize it as depression, I just knew something was really
wrong with me. I was willing to believe that I had a tumor or
cancer, because those types of physical illness were easy to
identify. I had some knowledge of cancer and tumors because I'd grown up in a home and in a society where those
types of illnesses were spoken about openly. One of my
grandfathers died of cancer, and the other died of diabetes
that was complicated by having various tumors in his body,
and during their illnesses I had heard my parents speak
openly about their prognoses. I had never heard my parents
talk about depression, or any other type of emotional illness.
Momi never referred to her low moods, we kids just knew

not to mess with her when she played her Billie Holiday albums, and Mama hummed spirituals all the time, but when she felt "troubled," as she'd say, she hummed louder. While I've always been keenly aware of my physical ailments, I didn't recognize the signs of my emotional pain because I didn't know what signs to look for in my life.

*What did your emotional pain look like, sis?*

*—Ella*

I was moody and irritable most of the time, and dissatisfied with my life, and I felt as if the world and everybody in it was against me. I couldn't sleep, or concentrate on anything for long periods. I'm normally a little anxious, but when I was depressed I found myself worrying all the time, only I couldn't explain what I worried about, and I just felt a general overall feeling of being unhappy, only I didn't know why I felt that way. Now, for me that was painful, because it wasn't normally the way I felt. It took going to the doctor for physical pain to find out that I was in emotional pain. I needed someone else to help me figure it out. Our bodies do give us signs of emotional pain, we just have to learn to recognize them as well as we recognize the signs for physical pain.

*I understand what you're sayin', sis, and I truly mean no disrespect, Cassie, because I remember when you were goin' through your rough times, and I want you to know that I prayed for you every day. But I still can't get away from a lot of this mental stuff bein' connected to a weakness in personal spirit. A lot of what you're sayin' makes sense, but it's just never been that way for me. I'm not 'shamed of feeling low sometimes but it's like they say, if you never have the down times how are you goin' to know what the up times look like? I think about my mother and grandmother and all those sistahs that came before us, they got through a lot tougher times than we'll ever see, and they didn't have anybody to talk to but each other and the good Lord. It worked for them and I guess it'll have to work for me too.*

*—Queenie*

*I don't take offense, Queenie, thanks for the prayers 'cause I sure did need them and besides I know you love me. I don't think I'm weak though, maybe I was before when I was doin' all that stuff, but not now. You may not believe this but I think it was my higher power that gave me the courage to ask for help when I did. Part of what I've been learning through my program is that drugs and alcohol will always be a part of my life, because there's a history in my family, but they don't have to be a necessary part of my life in order for me to cope with things. I also don't believe that my life has to be hard. There may be some hard times but I have the power to get through them just like I have the power to get through the good times. I think sis is right when she said that our bodies have different ways of telling us we're hurtin'. We just have to pay attention to the pain and stop tryin' to pretend it's not there.*

*—Cassie*

*I'm no expert but I don't think we ignore our pain, I just think we've gotten so used to doin' without, as far as medical attention is concerned, until we've learned how to work around the physical and mental pain. I'll admit I'm like Queenie. I get low sometimes, but I don't get low because I'm depressed, I get to feelin' that way 'cause I'm mad at the struggle that we have to go through as Black women just to get treated with any kind of respect. My mother taught me never let nobody see you cry; no matter how bad you're hurtin' just keep your head up; if you fall down, get up, brush yourself off, and keep right on going. It's not so much about hurtin' or weakness for me, it's a matter of personal pride.*

*—Eboni*

*I'll give an amen to that, 'cause I don't buy the personal weakness part either. I don't consider myself a weak person, and like I said before I get down every once in a while but I deal with it. We all have our own separate ways of dealin' with whatever kinds of pain we're in at the time, and some of us do better with it than others: Joyce has headaches, Cassie used to drink and drug, Eboni, you get mad, Queenie uses prayer, and most of the time I just wait it out. Would it cross my mind to kill myself, no I don't think so, but you can bet your bottom dollar if it did I'd be on somebody's couch in no time flat. To my way of thinkin' we don't have a problem thinkin' we're weak when we're sick with a cold or the flu, so why should something like this make us weak?*

*—Zoey*

*I think it's the mental thing that scares me, Zoey. I take a lot of pride in being able to hold my own. It's like if my mind's not working right what do I have left?*

*—Ella*

*Well, from what I've been hearin' there's no guarantee that your mind is workin' right if the rest of you isn't workin'.*

*—Zoey*

*Zoey, you just need to hush. I don't blame Ella one bit for bein' scared. I've been listenin' to what sis said about the mind and body connection, but it's a big leap from havin' a physical illness to havin' a mental illness. It's like Eboni said, if we can't get what we need when we're sick with something physical how do we know that we'll be any better off talkin' to somebody about what's goin' on in our head? My friend Jesse couldn't get any sleep after his father passed, so he went to see his doctor. His doctor sent him to a counselor—Jesse called him a shrink—but Jesse said the first thing that doctor wanted to know was all of his business and when he got done the doctor handed him a prescription for some pills. Jesse said he took that lil' piece of paper, balled it up, and threw it away. Jesse said that man musta thought he was crazy, but he knew that he was grievin' cause his father died, he didn't have some damn mental problem. See, that's what I'm talkin' about. Why should we go and talk to some stranger, puttin' all our business out in the street, 'cause you and I both know they talk about us Black folks anyway. Besides I just ain't all that comfortable talkin' to them folks.*

*—Flo*

*I don't mind talking with you all about how I'm feeling, but I'm not comfortable talking to strangers. Quiet as it's kept I don't even talk to my family all that much about how I'm feeling, 'cause I don't want them worrying about me. Besides, I'm not very good at taking advice, and I really don't think they're going to tell me anything new.*

*—Ella*

*My counselor didn't really give me advice, she pointed out a few things, some of which I already knew like how bad I was hurtin', and she helped me to develop new ways of coping with my stress.*

*—Cassie*

*See, that's just what I'm talkin' about. If you already had the answers, why pay somebody good money to tell you that you've got the answers? Hearin' some mess like that would really make me want to hurt somebody. Then I won't only need a counselor, I'd need a lawyer too.*

*—Flo*

I think what Cassie is saying is that when we're in crisis it's hard to sort out different information. Depression can make you doubt yourself big-time. I remember being so confused that I didn't know if I was coming or going. It felt good to talk to somebody who could be objective about my situation. You know we worry an awful lot about putting our business in the street, but what we fail to recognize is that when we're depressed we don't have to tell people our business, our mood and behaviors do that for us. It's like I've said before, our mind and bodies operate together, and when something is troubling us, it has a way of showing up. As someone who works in the field, I can't say that therapists don't discuss certain individual cases, we have to talk to doctors and other practitioners at times in order to coordinate care. But I can tell you this from my own experience, there are laws that we're required to follow concerning everybody's right to privacy, in and out of therapy sessions.

*Personally, I don't care if they tell Moses on the mount as long as they can help me if I need 'em.*

*—Zoey*

*Tell me this, sis, if you're in the business and you know all this stuff, what are you doin' gettin' depressed in the first place?*

—*Queenie*

I wasn't born a therapist, Queenie, in fact you all know that I always jokingly say that I became a therapist so that I would know when I was actually going crazy. Depression affects everybody, it doesn't care about profession, skin color, gender, or anything else. Everybody deals with stress on some level, even professionals in the field, and I'm no exception.

*I've been thinkin'. What if I go to my doctor and he does the same thing that Flo's friend's doctor did, you know, give me a prescription for pills. Like I said a while back, I don't know that I trust all that stuff like Prozac, it just scares me to think about taking something like that.*

—*Ella*

*I take medication for my depression, Ella, and like I told you it really helps me. Prozac isn't the only anti-depressant medication out there. The way I look at it, what's the difference between takin' medication for high blood pressure and takin' medication for depression? In fact, this issue wouldn't even come up if we were talkin' about takin' medication for somethin' physical.*

—*Cassie*

*I can tell you what the difference is for me, I know what the high blood pressure pills are doin' for my body, but I don't know what that other medication is supposes to be doin'. What do you think, sis?*

—*Flo*

Actually, I was thinking about the first time I had an asthma attack, and I had to be rushed to the hospital emergency room for a breathing treatment. After my treatment the doctor gave me a prescription for an asthma inhaler and told me to use it whenever I felt an asthma attack coming on. I filled the prescription, but by then I was feeling better so I took the inhaler and put it in my bathroom medicine cabinet. The next time I had an asthma attack I went back to the emergency room, got another breathing treatment, and the doctor gave me another prescription for another inhaler. I guess he thought I had lost the first one; he never asked and I never said. Anyway, I did the same thing with the second inhaler that I did with the first one, threw it in the medicine cabinet. So about two months later I had another really bad asthma attack and I went back to the emergency room for yet another breathing treatment. This time the doctor asked me if the inhalers were working and I told him I didn't know because I'd never used them. At first he looked surprised and then he pulled up a chair and calmly said, "Let me explain what happens with your lungs when you have an asthma attack." He then went on to explain and he showed me how the inhaler could help me to get some relief. He asked if I would be willing to try using the inhaler the next time I felt an asthma attack coming on and he asked me to call him and tell him if I noticed any difference. I've been using my inhaler from that day to this, whenever I feel an asthma attack coming on. What I recognized is that before the doctor gave me information I was unwilling to trust his direction. After he shared information with me, I was more willing to try the medication. I guess I don't think taking medication as it's prescribed is right or wrong. I think of medication as a tool that we can use when all of our other tools stop working.

We also have the option of using natural herbal remedies, similar in many ways to the things our mothers and grandmothers gave us. In the case of depression many health care professionals are recommending trying hypericum or, as it's commonly known, St. John's wort. While St. John's wort can't be prescribed for depression in the traditional sense, because of FDA (Food and Drug Administration) standards and other reasons, it's been used for the treatment of mild to moderate depression in Germany and throughout Europe for years, with a great deal of success. Within the last year, as it's gotten more exposure through the media, St. John's wort taken in 300 mg doses three times a day has proven to be very effective and has gained a strong, steady following in the United States.

I also believe that information is power, and when I have information I can make the decision that feels right for me. I don't truly believe that anybody can make us do anything, including using medication. Think about it, when was the last time someone made you do something against your will? I think that doctors or counselors can present the option of using medication, and give you clear information so that you can make an informed decision as to whether or not you'd like to try the medication.

*I guess I'm not sure that medication would be the answer for me, if I'm depressed. I might be willing to see somebody if I knew there were other options available to me. I'm just not sure that I would be willing to take something, not right now anyway.*

*—Ella*

There are several treatment options for depression, Ella, of which medication is one. Research done by the National Institute of Mental Health shows that often medication coupled with therapy has proven to be one of the most effective treatments. But a lot depends on the causes (there's often more than one) of your depression and the length of time you've been depressed. The best thing to do is talk with a doctor or counselor so that you can get a proper assessment.

One of the things that I'm aware of is that when I'm in good physical condition, it helps me to handle emotional stress better. That's one of the reasons I enjoy working out.

*How will exercise help? Maybe if I start doing something like that first. . . .*

*—Ella*

*You know, Ella, I just started doin' something that might interest you. I've just started takin' this meditation and yoga class over at the community college, and I've only had a couple of classes but I'm really gettin' into it. All the stretching and breathing exercises really help you to get in touch with your body in a more spiritual way. One of the strong points for me is that it allows me to focus and train my thinking, and at the same time I'm working on my body, but not in*

*the fall-out, fall-down physical sense. I can't stand doing all*
*that jumpin' and runnin' around they do at the gym.*

*—Cassie*

I tend to think of exercise as part of the prevention process. It doesn't necessarily cure what's wrong but it can help us to mentally and physically feel better. Our bodies need a certain amount of activity in order to work properly. I know it sounds odd but our bodies need energy in order to produce more energy. Whenever I start feeling slowed down or sluggish, I think of it as my body's way of saying "Look'a here, girlfriend, if you want me to keep going then you better give me an energy boost." The exercise we choose for ourselves doesn't have to be something that inspires a video workout tape. That's why I personally enjoy walking, it's simple and the only thing it really requires is time.

*Well, I don't always feel like one hundred percent, but for me*
*I think age has a lot to do with it. My mother, bless her heart,*
*lived to the ripe old age of ninety-eight and I fully expect*
*to do the same. It's just a natural fact that the body wears*
*out after a period of time, gettin' old is a fact of life. I go to*
*the doctor if I have to, but these tired old bones been doin'*
*fine for a long time, and I expect they'll continue on till they*
*give out.*

*—Queenie*

I personally believe that the aging process is normal, and the changing of life that occurs as we grow older doesn't have to equal the breakdown of life. The natural aging process that our bodies experience need not include the emotional process of depression. Tina Turner is my personal role model when I look at aging. That sistah has it going on in the looks and energy department, plus she's emotionally fit as well. Tina's comfortable with her life and it shows in the way that she presents herself.

*Yeah, I'd be comfortable with myself too, if I had Tina's money*
*and lifestyle. I think it's easy for people with money to tell us*
*what they're doing with their lives, but it just don't fit for most*
*of us everyday folks. Sometimes I read those magazines*

*and think to myself, well, why shouldn't they lose a hundred pounds or be in excellent shape; if I had a personal cook to plan my meals and a trainer I'd be in excellent shape too. Let's get real, those folks have nannies, grannies, and everybody else waitin' on them hand and foot. As soon as I get rich and famous I'ma have folks plannin' my days and waitin' on me too. But right about now it's easier said than done.*

*—Flo*


*I heard that, Flo! I know just what you mean, cause every time I read about this star doin' this and that I think to my-self, well, why shouldn't they be havin a good life. I mean, I don't begrudge them their success or nothing like that, but it's like, damn, they don't have to worry about the things that we have to worry 'bout like payin' light bills or dealin' with day care. Shoot, sometimes I think the only reason I don't do drugs is 'cause I can't afford them. I'm lyin', that ain't why I don't do drugs, but the rest is for real. I heard this interview with Janet Jackson and she was talkin' about how she's been dealin' with this deep depression and I'm sittin' there and thinkin' to myself, girl, what in the world you got to be depressed 'bout? You got it all: a body that won't quit, money, and you can get any man out there, so what's the problem?*

*—Eboni*

I know where you're coming from, I read those maga-zines too. And it does look like the so-called superstars have it all, but I also know that they're women just like we are. Although the same types of things that get us down may not affect them in the same way, that doesn't mean that they don't deal with their own demons, of which depression might be one. I ain't gonna sit here and lie, having money in the bank makes life a whole lot easier to deal with, but it doesn't mean we wouldn't have things in our lives that would still bring us down. After seeing the Jackson story on HBO a couple of years ago, I'm not surprised that Janet Jackson deals with depression from time to time. It looked to me like her father could be pretty abusive and she had to compete with her brothers just to be recognized by her family members. That kind of stuff affects a person's self-esteem, and money doesn't erase those types of thoughts or memories. Look at Phyliss Hyman, she had fame and fortune too, and she committed suicide because she didn't think she was good enough. I know that it seems like we get depressed because we don't have certain things in our lives, but really it's more about how we view our lives as a whole. If we only look at what we don't have we're always going to be depressed, but if we can look at one thing about ourselves and honestly like what we see, then chances are even on our down days we won't stay down for long.

*It seems to me that we forget that those folks that made it have to work twice as hard to keep it, know what I mean? A personal trainer can help the stars work their bodies, but they have to take care of workin' their minds. I think the name of the game is what ya gonna do for you. Personally I've gotten off into the whole health food, natural vitamins thing. I still go to the doctor's but since I've started using vitamins and watching what I eat it seems like I don't have to go as often.*

—Zoey

*Yeah, now all you have to do is work on givin' up smokin' them nasty cigarettes.*

—Queenie

*I hear you, Queenie, and I'm workin' on it, as a matter of fact I just got one of those stop smokin' kits yesterday.*

—Zoey

Sometimes doing just one thing differently can have a positive impact on our mood: going for a walk, changing a habit, talking to someone you trust in or out of the medical community, going to the gym, and yes, even taking medication. We have a long history of suspicions and fears connected to the medical profession, and with good cause given this country's history of racism, sexism, and unequal access; however, over the years many things have changed. Are things perfect in the medical community? No, they are not, but we have the power of choice today that our foremothers didn't have and when a medical professional or service doesn't fit our needs we can make another choice. We often think of medicine in terms of tonics, pills, and potions, and while they can and do serve a very valuable and important place in our need for health care, the most potent medicine is always going to be preventive self-care.

## Recognizing Our Thought Patterns

We often don't recognize how closely our thoughts are connected to our mood. When we have a pleasant thought it puts us in a pleasant mood, and when we have an unpleasant thought it causes an unpleasant mood. When we're depressed we have an overabundance of unpleasant or negative thoughts that bring our mood down. Our negative thoughts tend to be very personal, and very powerful, often going unnoticed and unchallenged because we don't recognize them for what they are . . . emotional hostage keepers. When we can see and put our negative thoughts to the reality test, we discover that they often fail to meet the challenge of being factually based. The following pages contain exercises that will help you to challenge your negative thoughts by giving you the power to recognize which thoughts are your personal emotional hostage keepers. By testing how often these negative thoughts occur for you, you will have the option of restructuring your thoughts in order to experience a change in your mood.

I would suggest making copies of the following pages in order to create worksheets, so you can practice the exercises on a daily basis.

## Emotional Hostage Keepers (Negative Automatic Thoughts)

**Labeling and mislabeling:** This generally occurs when there's a problem and you attach a negative label to yourself: "I'm a failure," or "I'm a screw up." *Mislabeling* is when someone else does something that you disagree with, and in anger you label the individual: "She's so stupid," or "She's a fool."

**Disqualifying the positive:** You reject your positive experiences as if they don't count. "I didn't do anything special, anybody could have done it," or "If they really knew me they wouldn't think I'm so smart."

**Mental filter:** You select a negative detail and dwell on it over and over until it colors your entire perception of the event. "Everyone said it was a good party, but then I spilled the punch all over the floor. I ruined the party for everybody."

**Jumping to conclusions:** You give something a negative interpretation before the facts are known. "It was an okay interview, but I know I won't get the job."

**Overgeneralization:** You turn a single negative event into an overall statement about yourself. "I forgot to put gas in the car; I never do anything right."

**Emotional reasoning:** You base everything on your negative emotions. "I feel like she doesn't like me." You feel it, therefore it's a fact.

**Personalization:** You see yourself as being responsible for some unrelated negative event over which you don't have control. "He wouldn't have had that wreck if I hadn't lent him my car."

**"Should" and "If only" statements:** You hold yourself an emotional hostage and blame yourself with statements that make you feel guilty. "I should have been there for her," or "If only I had been a better wife, mother, lover."

**All or nothing thinking:** You lock yourself into seeing things in one of two ways, right or wrong, without leaving any middle ground, often believing that you have to be perfect or else you've failed. "Why couldn't I get all A's?"

**Catastrophizing:** You exaggerate your mistakes, often making them more important than they actually are in context to the situation. "I can't believe I screwed up in such a big way," or "I've really blown it now."

## Emotional Hostage Keepers

Recognizing our hostage-keeping negative thoughts is the first step in being able to challenge them. On the previous page there was a list of the ten most common hostage keepers. Read through the list carefully and identify the negative thoughts that most often hold you hostage. On this page write down your five most commonly used negative thoughts, numbering them in order of their frequency.

Mon.  Tue.  Wed.  Thurs.  Fri.  Sat.  Sun.

1. _____
2. _____
3. _____
4. _____
5. _____

For the next week notice how often these negative thoughts come up for you. Each time you notice the thought, put a mark by it under the corresponding day, for example:

Mon.

1. Emotional reasoning          *////*

This exercise will help you to notice which particular hostage keepers are causing you the most difficulty.

## Mental Rehearsal

Often our negative thoughts are triggered by events or situations that occur during our day-to-day experiences. Something will happen, for example an unpleasant confrontation with a coworker, and we'll respond in a certain way. Due to the unpleasantness of the situation we may find ourselves replaying the event over and over in our minds, often wondering if we could have handled it differently. This exercise will allow you to step back from the situation and practice a different reaction for possible future use. This exercise will take about twenty minutes.

Find a quiet place where you won't be interrupted for about twenty minutes and get comfortable.

Close your eyes and *see* the situation.
Notice *yourself* in the situation.
What are you *doing*? What are you *thinking*?

Now open your eyes, take a deep breath, exhale, and . . .

Close your eyes again and *see* the situation.
Notice *yourself* in the situation, *behaving differently.*
What are you *doing*? What are you *thinking*?
What do you *notice*? What's your *experience* now?

You can also use this exercise to mentally rehearse upcoming events and situations that might prove to be stressful.

# The Love's Gone Wrong Blues

## FAST FACTS
▼▲▼▲▼

Women are more likely to suffer from depression following the breakup of a relationship.

Women tend to view themselves as failures when a relationship doesn't work out.

Society places more pressure on women to be in relationships.

## DELLA'S STORY

*Frankie and I split up four months ago today, and it still feels like it just happened. I never thought I'd have such a rough time dealing with her leaving, but it's still fresh. We'd been together five years and she just decides she wants out. This is the woman that I thought I was going to grow old with, and all of a sudden she wants more space. Just doesn't make any sense to me. I could see it if we weren't good together, but she was my soulmate. Even now I cry sometimes when I think about her. I always seem to pick the wrong kind of person, maybe I have a sign on my head that says use me, 'cause it sure feels that way. I should have known something was up, though, 'cause she had started staying out late, and going back to the clubs, but whenever I would try to ask her anything she would just clam up and accuse me of being insecure and possessive. Hell, I just thought I was being concerned and loving. She's always been independent, in fact, that's why I was attracted to her in the first place. I don't know, maybe I was being possessive and insecure. I don't feel like I know anything anymore. When she first left I thought I was going crazy. I was calling her all the time, I even went to the center where she works trying to get her to talk to me, but then she got a restraining order against me and that blew me away. I'm not a violent person and she knows that, although there was that one time when she made me mad and I pushed her outta my face, but that happened a long time ago. I'm forty-two years old, I don't want to go through life alone.*

## DIAMOND'S STORY

*Leon and I have been separated for six months now and I'm still havin' a hard time dealin' with it. I love him but I just couldn't put up with his drinkin' and runnin' the streets anymore. I know I did the right thing in leavin' him, but the truth is, most days I just operate on automatic pilot, goin' through the motions of life but not really feelin' like I have a life. Right about now work is my only savin' grace, because it gives me an excuse not to think about everything else. I haven't told anybody about what's happenin' with me and*

*Leon because I don't want them in my business, so I just put on my best face and carry on like everything is all right with the world. Leon called me last night, he says he wants to work things out, but I've heard that before. He's good at giving lip service, but piss-poor at follow through, and I'm just tired of strugglin' with tryin' to make him understand how his foolishness is hurtin' me and the kids. Our family means the world to me, and I know he loves us too, but I just can't deal anymore. I tried talking to my mother the other night about how I was feelin' and she just gave me her standard answer, "Just give it to the Lord, baby, just give it to the Lord." I was so fed up at that point I just burst out crying and told her that I did give it to the Lord and he gave it back. I don't know, sometimes I feel as if I'm bein' punished, but I don't know what I've done to deserve it. I've tried to lead a good life, I go to church, raise my kids right, and have a halfway decent job. I'm a strong Black woman, I'm not used to feeling this way. I screwed up my courage the other night and told my sister that I thought I was depressed and I was thinking about seeing somebody. She told me that I just needed to stop feeling sorry for myself, 'cause our mama didn't raise no fools and if Leon wanted to act crazy, I should just divorce him and get on with my life. I don't know, maybe she's right, maybe I am feelin' sorry for myself. I just hate to think that I've failed at my marriage, that's all. I want my kids to have their daddy and I want my husband, but right about now I don't know what's worse, the pain of bein' with him or the pain of bein' without him.*

M y grief was just about over, or so I thought. I still had crying jags, and sleeping was fitful, but for the most part I felt on the mend. We had been together three years and the breakup several months prior was unexpected, although we had separated countless times over the years. For whatever reason, this one had the true feel of finality. Our recent conversations always seemed to end with his statement of wanting something different and not really knowing what different actually was, but he seemed clear in not wanting us to be together. I wasn't as clear about wanting things to end, although I knew for months that things weren't right between us. But I'm a fighter by nature and in my mind I was sure we could work out whatever was getting in the way of our happiness as a couple. I wanted to hold on but he was letting go, and the emotional roller coaster of up and down feelings was taking a toll on my mental and physical health. I suffered from all the signs of being "released from love": restless sleep, uncontrollable fits of tears, pulling away from friends and loved ones, not eating, and feeling helplessly alone in a world full of people. Even now in thinking about it I find myself replaying our final time together as if it was the ending scene in some Old World–style, tragic romantic love story.

Without a doubt, and notwithstanding the death of a loved one, or a life threatening illness the breakup of an intimate relationship is the worst type of human pain and suffering an individual is ever asked to face in a lifetime. The sadness, tears, and feelings of loss are overwhelming and, coupled with the memories and thoughts of what could have been different, are enough to tear down even the toughest show of emotional strength. Rejection of any kind is rough, but the emotional intensity of a rejection of love is the mother of all negative feelings rolled into one: hurt, anger, despair, emptiness, vulnerability, and fear all wrapped in one shaky package. I can remember right after my divorce I took a silent vow swearing off all men. That vow lasted all of six months. After my second attempt at a long-term relationship failed I swore off relationships and that vow lasted two months. That time I decided to swear off of swearing off and still found myself in breakup, breakdown city. I couldn't hide from the enormously overpowering thought that I was somehow responsible for the failure of the relationships that had occurred in my life.

"Zoey, what's wrong with me? Why can't I get it right?"

"I didn't notice you doin' anything wrong."

"Why do I keep picking men who can't commit?"

"Sounds to me like it's the guys who have the problem, not you."

"It must be something I'm doing wrong, otherwise this wouldn't be happening to me."

"Well, the last time I checked, it's kind of hard to make somebody do somethin' they're not ready to do. My mother always told me that the only time you could change somebody was when they were in diapers. And unless you've been robbin' some big-time cradles, I'm thinkin' that those guys just weren't ready for the same thing that you were ready for."

"Yeah, but why do I keep pickin' those type of guys? I mean it works for a while, and then they just want to give up."

"Well, unless they've got the word 'non-commitment' tattooed on their forehead, how would you know that you're choosin' the wrong kind of guy? After all, sweetcakes, it wasn't your decision to leave, it was their decision, know what I mean?"

"But I can't seem to get over the thought that I did something wrong."

"The only thing that you did wrong, sweetcakes, was blame yourself for another person's decision. It hurts 'cause rejection is suppose to hurt, but bein' hurt doesn't mean it was your fault. Sometimes when we hold on too long, it only makes the hurt that much stronger."

One of the things that I truly love about Zoey, other than the fact that she's Zoey, of course, is her ability to cut through the b.s. and get straight to the heart of the matter. She was right, the depression I found myself experiencing was directly related to the misbelief that I was somehow responsible for someone else's decision. I wasn't holding on to the relationship, that was gone—I was holding on to the pain that was associated with the belief that I had somehow "failed" to do something right. I found myself caught in the trap that many of us find ourselves in when we experience rejection, the trap of helplessness. I believed I could fix the situation by fixing me; however, as Zoey pointed out, I wasn't broken. I was emotionally wounded and I had the nasty habit of picking at the scab, preventing it from healing. As the days turned into weeks, I found myself turning the pain rejection into a noble venture of misery. I couldn't get away from assigning blame, blame for the breakup, blame for not doing "it" right, blame for not being good enough, strong enough or right enough to stop the inevitable, someone else's decision. The more I picked at the scab of rejection the worse I felt, and the dangerous infection of depression soon set in. As the weeks slowly dragged by, and I had the chance to gain a better sense of emotional distance between myself and my pain, I found myself taking a mental inventory of the beliefs I held regarding relationships. I believed that it was my responsibility to somehow make the relationship work. This was a nice belief, and I liked it because it gave me a sense of control. Being somewhat of a control freak I felt that if I could control the relationship, I could control the outcome, but as some nice beliefs have a way of doing, it failed to pass the reality check. In reality I alone couldn't control the relationship, no matter how much responsibility I took on. Two people were involved and two people had to be responsible for the outcome. My other belief of having to assign blame for the breakup of the relationship also failed the reality check. People leave relationships for a variety of reasons, and unless there's a clear case of abuse, it's really not useful to hold ourselves or the other person hostage. I was certain that my ex-partner and I wouldn't be bosom buddies, but I didn't need him as my lifelong enemy. As I allowed myself to go through and take stock of my belief inventory, I discovered that a couple of revisions were in order. The rejection and subsequent depression I felt were indeed real, and again as Zoey pointed out, I hurt because rejection is designed to hurt. However, I discovered an important lesson in this healing process that I had overlooked in my previous relationship breakups. I found that my beliefs about the breakup were directly related to the speed of my healing process. The hurt, sadness, and anger that I felt were still present; however, there was an absence of guilt. I no longer felt the heavy pressure of believing that there had to be blame, in order to justify my reality of pain.

*I remember when I broke up with Martin I thought it was for the best, honey, it nearly drove me outta my mind. I knew I was doin' the right thing, but it still felt like the wrong thing. It was my decision to leave him, and I still had all those same feelin's that you had. I thought once I had his sorry butt outta my life, I would feel better, but for a while there, I was ready to give it another try just to stop from feelin' so damn bad.*

*—Eboni*

Choosing to leave a relationship doesn't mean that we get to escape our feelings. Hurting on some level is a natural part of the separation process. It doesn't matter who makes the decision to leave, rejection is always painful. It's how we deal with our thoughts about the breakup that makes the difference. I'm always amazed at how some folks walk away from one relationship and into another without taking time to process their feelings. When a person jumps from one relationship to the next they carry all of their feelings of hurt and pain with them. This type of dirty emotional baggage can put an awful strain on the next intimate encounter. I also find myself worrying about the person who puts on the brave show of an "I ain't hurtin'," type of attitude, because their emotional pain will often get misplaced in an unhealthy manner.

*You know, the main reason I think I don't get too involved with anybody is because I don't want to deal with the pain of breaking up, and it always happens at some point down the line.*

*—Ella*

*I don't know about that, Ella, me and James have been together almost fifteen years, and yeah we have our ups and downs but we hang in there. Being with someone doesn't mean that you'll break up, not all the time anyway.*

*—Lyndey*

*Amen to that bit of news, Willie and I have been together for goin' on eight years and sometimes it surprises me that we've lasted as long as we have, but I believe that you have to have a certain mind-set in order to make it. Lord knows neither one of us is perfect, but we just look past the bad things and stay focused on what's good about each other and that seems to get us through.*

*—Queenie*

I believe that relationships can be very positive experiences. It's like Queenie says, we have to have a certain mind-set about the type of expectations we have going into the relationship. If we go into a relationship believing that it's going to fail and that we're going to be hurt, then those things will more than likely occur. But if we allow ourselves to believe that we can be flexible, then we have a better chance of making it in a relationship.

*Wait a minute, a little bit ago Zoey said that we can't change the other person, and we shouldn't blame ourselves if things don't work out, so which is it? I just want to meet somebody and settle down, but it's like Ella said, half the time when you meet somebody, they're not interested in being straight up, they just want to play stupid head games. It's easier not to be bothered, than it is to be hurt.*

*—Joyce*

We don't have the power to change another person; however, we do have the power to change how we view ourselves in relation to another person. Having a relationship go bad doesn't mean that we've failed or that we can't ever have a fulfilling relationship, it just means that for whatever reason that particular union didn't work out for us. When I hear sisters say things like, "It's easier not to get involved because I don't want to get hurt," or some version of "there's just no good brothers available," it leads me to think that the sisters may have some unrealistic beliefs about their own sense of personal power within a relationship.

*Well, I don't personally think it's unrealistic not to want to be dogged out, cheated on, or lied to in a relationship, and so far those are the things that broke up all the other relationships I was in. I want to meet someone who wants the same kinds of things I want in life. You know, the simple things like mutual respect for each other, having a family, the whole nine yards, but I just can't seem to meet those types of men.*

*—Joyce*

I agree one hundred percent, Joyce; when you've had all of those things happen it can make it difficult to get close; however, you didn't cause those things to happen, and you certainly didn't choose the men you were with because you expected them to do those things in the relationship. The other side of the coin is that not all men do those things, and there are still decent brothers out there who believe as you do, that a relationship is about respect.

I also believe that our selection process is governed by what and how we think a person will behave in a relationship. While it makes sense to be cautious in regards to choosing a soulmate, if we close our mind to the fact that not all men operate in a dishonest way, then we close off the chance of meeting a nice brother to settle down with in a relationship.

*I remember when I met Donny, it was like I went out with him a couple of times, and I thought, this brother is just too laid back for me. I mean he's quiet and doesn't say a whole lot, and he's a fighter but in a different way, he fights with reason and logic and he doesn't try to force his opinion off on me. Now that was really different. Martin and I used to go round for round, sometimes fist to fist; it was like everything had to be his way. It took me a while to understand how Donny dealt with things, and because I'd gotten so used to havin' to fight about everythin' I kept expectin' Donny to be the same way. But now I kinda like the fact that we can talk instead of arguin' and fightin' all the time. I still blow up every now and again but he just refuses to get hooked. I'm really glad I decided to give him more of a chance.*

*—Eboni*

I've discovered that by giving myself permission to be open in meeting a lot of different types of men, I'm really starting to meet more men. The more men I meet the greater my chances are of coming in contact with someone who shares my values regarding being in a relationship. I believe that as women we often put a lot of unreal demands on our partners, such as the belief that "this person will make me happy" or "this person will fill all of my needs in terms of love, and friendship." When we go into a relationship with those types of thoughts we often end up feeling disappointed and hurt when we discover that the person can't live up to our expectations. So often we get stuck in wanting to find out what the other person has to offer, and forget to look at what we have to bring to the union. We have to start asking ourselves some important questions in regards to our wanting to be in a relationship, questions like:

How would this person complement my life?
What can I bring to this relationship as an individual?
What do I really need in terms of time commitment?
Will a relationship with this person allow me the room I
  need to pursue my individual interests?
Am I in a position to commit the time and energy
  needed to develop the type of relationship I want
  to have?

And the most important question of all:

What are my expectations of this person in terms of
  commitment?

When we can ask ourselves these types of questions and give ourselves honest answers, then we're on the right track.

*Even when you do all that stuff, asking the questions and stuff, things can still not work out. You can still end up getting hurt.*

*—Ella*

That's true, we can do all that we know how to do and the relationship still may not work out the way we would like; however, we can take some comfort in knowing that we tried our best.

*Do what I do, Ella, just think of that relationship that doesn't work as practice. When I broke up with Anna, I just kept dating and when I met a woman that I liked but it didn't work out I just told myself that one was practice for the real thing. It's kind of different in that I had to look at having a whole new circle of friends, 'cause all of the women I was used to meeting were into the drugs and alcohol lifestyle. When I look at things that don't work out as practice, then I don't beat up on myself as much. This frame of mind lets me be more relaxed when I'm meeting people.*

*—Cassie*

Believing that we have to have a relationship puts us in the position of feeling vulnerable, and that creates unneeded tension. Rejecting that belief takes the pressure off and allows us to open ourselves up to more pleasurable experiences with people. Being relaxed gives us the emotional space to get to know and appreciate another person. It's important to remember that the best relationships are developed from friendships. And most friendships are rooted in respect and trust, which can expand into a mutual love for each other. Unfortunately, life rarely if ever has fairy tale endings, which means that even people who love each other can grow apart at some point, and while we can't always avoid the pain involved in the breakup of a relationship, we can make a choice as to how we deal with that pain. Holding ourselves responsible for another person's choice to leave places us in the position of believing that we've failed. It's important to remember that loving someone, no matter what the outcome, is never a failure, it's a gift.

# Going for the Goal

Action is more important than motivation.

Accomplishing small daily goals helps us feel
successful.

Break down problems into small manageable
steps.

## ERICA'S STORY

*My friends at school say I'm depressed, but personally I just think they're jealous because I take my studies so seriously. They don't seem to understand that I want to be taken seriously, because I want people's respect. I want everybody to understand that just because I'm young, Black, and female I'm not a failure. I take a lot of pride in my studies. I was sixth in my graduating high school class; I should've been number one, but that month that I was out sick really threw my GPA off. I get good grades now, but I have to work my butt off to keep them. I wish I could breeze through my studies like some of these kids, but it just takes me longer. I'm proud of the fact that I get good grades, I just wish I could do better is all. If I can do a halfway decent job I have a pretty good chance of getting into pre-med and that's all I've dreamed about. I wish I could be more popular like my friends, more laid back and less "intense," as my friend Paula says, but I don't want to take a chance and mess up. I can't afford to let my guard down or I'll never be able to get back on track. Paula and those other guys are going to end up chasing some dude to the altar and having a ton of babies. My friend Renee says I don't have a sense of humor, but I just fail to see what's funny about not having a decent career. I want a boyfriend and all, but my studies have to come first that's all there is to it. I can always have fun later. I expect a lot of myself but that's not a bad thing; in fact, I happen to think it's the only way to get ahead. Shoot, half of these guys won't even finish the term, so I can't see where they have room to talk about me.*

> When we fail to plan, we plan to fail.
> —Highway billboard

I used to believe that I was a list-maker by nature, but when I think about it, I grew up in a home where the phrase "Write it down" was as common as "Don't eat in the living room." Momi was big on making lists for everything from shopping to household chores. I used to think that Daddy was born with a pencil wedged behind his ear, and

Mama's (my grandmother's) favorite saying was "A short pencil beats a long memory every time." So it fits to some degree that list-making is a part of my nature. As an adult I recognize that my list-making abilities serve as my daily action plan, and I have to admit I get a certain amount of satisfaction from putting a big bold line through a finished task.

*Maybe I'm a little slow, but what's this got to do with depression?*

*—Flo*

Well, one of the things I've noticed is that it's easy to feel discouraged and down on ourselves when we believe that we haven't been able to fulfill our lifelong dreams. We grow up hearing that we should have goals, and that it's important to have a master plan, but it's rare that anyone ever tells us how to put together an action plan for achieving our life goals. I once heard a great motivational speaker say, "Always reach for the moon, but remember you've got to do it one star at a time." If the moon is our goal, then the stars are our action plan, one leads us to the other. I personally don't believe that we ever fail at anything, but I do think that we sometimes forget to lay out a plan for making what we want to happen in our lives, happen.

*So you're sayin' that we need to sit down and write out a list every time we want to do somethin'. I hear where you're comin' from, but what's the chances of bein' able to do that all the time?*

*—Joyce*

*I heard that. Half the time I don't know where I'm goin' till I get there. The kids have a joke 'round the house when I'm lookin' for somethin' or I can't remember somethin'. They say, "Uh oh, Mom's in a state of terminal confusion again."*

*—Flo*

I like that phrase, "state of terminal confusion," because that's just where we mentally and emotionally end up when we neglect to make a plan for ourselves. Making lists may seem impractical on the surface, but in reality we do it all the time in our minds. Think about the times you've said to yourself, "I've got to remember to . . ." then you go off and get busy doing something else and forget what it is that you want to remember. I don't know about anybody else but when I forget to do something, I worry, and that worry leads to anxiety and the next thing I know I'm mentally holding myself hostage, saying things to myself like, "How could I be so dumb," or "I never do anything right." Neither of these two statements are true, but the minute I tell myself these things I start feeling bad, and if we feel bad long enough it can lead to being depressed.

*I used to have this dream of opening my own multicultural preschool. The head teacher at the Children's Center, where I work, even said that I'm a natural when it comes to working with the kids. Actually, that's the only time when I feel really good about myself, when I'm workin' with the kids, it's like I can really relate to them. But to be real honest I don't think makin' a list is gonna be real helpful in my case.*

*—Eboni*

*It's true, Eboni, Jamie loves being in your class. He always talks about "Auntie Eboni said" this or that. Maybe you should look into openin' your own school.*

*—Lyndey*

*I haven't really given up on the idea, but it's like time and money always seem to get in the way. Goin' back to school takes money, and that's somethin' that's always in short supply in my life. It's not just the money, though. There's just so much stuff involved, even thinkin' 'bout it makes me dizzy.*

*—Eboni*

It's like the motivational speaker said, Eboni, "We have to build our journey to the moon one star at a time." That means breaking down your dream into doable pieces, and the first step might be sitting down and organizing your thoughts on a sheet of paper. Using a simple check-off list can help us to remember everyday tasks, but I like to use a different type of list to help me reach larger goals. Here's an example of how I put together that list.

## Main Goal
## Multicultural Preschool

Steps I need to take:
1. Go Back to School
2. Money
3. Time

What do I need in order to complete each step:

Step 1: School
- A. information about school programs
- B. talk to school advisor
- C. make a decision

Step 2: Money
- A. talk to someone at bank or credit union
- B. fill out applications
- C. turn in applications

Step 3: Time
- A. set aside one hour each day for this task
- B. 7–8 p.m. mark this time down
- C. do task

How will I reward myself for completing each phase of a step?
1. Give myself a word of encouragement
2. Buy myself flowers

Who will be my support through this process?

1. _____

2. _____

What distractions might get in the way of my completing these tasks?

How will I get myself back on track?

Each step of the process is built on a little list; however, each list puts you a little closer to completing your goal. When we put our thoughts down in an orderly fashion it helps us to cut down on that sense of terminal confusion that comes from being overwhelmed with information overload.

*I think this all sounds well and good, but what happens when you set the goal, make the plan, and it still doesn't happen? I worked my butt off for five years in order to put myself through school, and I graduated three years ago, thinking that I'd be at least an associate partner by now, but I'm still a sales rep. I work just as hard as everybody else, if not harder, but I still haven't made the grade. When I started at the firm five years ago they told me I'd have a better chance of moving up when I got my degree, they even helped me pay for my last two years of school. Well, I got my degree, and I'm only one level above where I was when I started. Sometimes I feel like what's the use? I might as well be working at the post office.*

*—Ella*

*Excuse me!! But the last time I checked, workin' at the post office beat the hell outta bein' on the street. I may not have no fancy degree, but I got a steady roof over my head, you know what I'm sayin'?*

*—Flo*

*I'm sorry, Flo, I didn't mean to go there, but sometimes I get so frustrated with myself because I have such a love/hate relationship with that job. It's like, I love all the perks, and my coworkers are great, but I hate the fact that I just can't seem to advance no matter what I do. Every time a top position opens up I apply, only to get my feelings hurt by watching them go outside and hire somebody else to fill the slot.*

*—Ella*

*Maybe it's time you start redesigning your goal plan, sweet-cakes. If you can't get what you want there, maybe you can get it somewhere else. Shoot, if they don't recognize how good you are, somebody else will. See, I think plannin' and settin' goals is all well and good, but when the power is in somebody else's hands all the goal settin' in the world may not change a thing. I'd be depressed too, if I had to sit and watch somebody else come in and steal my thunder.*

*—Zoey*

*I've thought about leaving a couple of times, but it would just mean starting all over from scratch. You know the drill, working like hell to prove yourself and all. Besides I'm over forty, and going into another company would mean losing my retirement and all the other benefits I've built up over the past five years. It may not seem like much but I've earned it, and I want to keep it.*

—Ella

I hear what you're saying, Ella, and I think you're right. On one level it sounds like you've certainly paid your dues. But I've been wondering if you've checked out how long it took the other associates to get their positions. If it took them longer, maybe you might need to readjust your timeline. If it took them a shorter period of time, then maybe it might be a good idea to realistically consider your options by asking yourself a few questions:

Do I enjoy enough of my current position to offset the
    parts of the position that displease me?
What do I have to gain by staying in this position?
What am I willing to give up by leaving this position?
If I stay, how will I take care of myself emotionally, men-
    tally, and physically?

Write the questions down and write out your answers so that you can go back to them from time to time over the next few days. I agree with Zoey when she talks about others having the power to affect whether or not we achieve our goals. Unfortunately, we don't live in a perfect, or even a "fair" society. However we can always take back our power by redefining the goal.

*Shoot, if it was me I'd slap the suckers with a lawsuit so fast it'd make their heads swim.*

—Eboni

*Eboni, darlin', if the laws worked in our favor, she wouldn't need to go that route in the first place, know what I'm sayin'?*

—Zoey

Going the legal route is always an option, but again, there aren't any hard and fast guarantees. The strongest power we have in achieving our dreams is our own power.

Someone once said the sweetest revenge in the world is the revenge of being successful. No one gives us success, we make our success by setting a goal, planning the action, and taking the steps to achieve the goal.

*I believe in settin' goals but I also believe in havin' a little luck along the way. I didn't finish high school, but as luck would have it my cousin told me they were hirin' down at the post office. I went down, took the test, and passed it, and I've been there ever since, it'll be fifteen years in March. By rights, I shouldn't even have a job, much less one that let's me make eighteen dollars an hour. Now that may not seem like a lot to some folks, but I can't go anywhere else and make that kind of money. And I did that without havin' a goal or plan. I'm not sayin' it's the best job in the world, but it keeps me and mine taken care of.*

*—Flo*

I believe in luck too, but the truth is luck is as fickle as anything else in the world. You got your job because you were qualified. You've been there fifteen years due to the fact that you work hard and earn every dollar you're paid. That may not seem like a goal, but the fact that you've been there that long tells me that this wasn't a lucky decision on your part. When we rely on luck it opens the door for us to discount the amount of work, time, and energy we put into a given project.

*Well, now, I don't know about that, 'cause I really feel lucky sometimes, like the time I won that two hundred dollars playin' bingo. I just knew I was gonna win somethin' and sure 'nough it happened. I didn't plan that and I couldn't't've known I was gonna win, so it had to be luck.*

*—Queenie*

It's not that good or unexpected things don't happen occasionally, it's just that I prefer to think that at those times we're feeling more optimistic or hopeful. When we have a more optimistic outlook on things we feel better about ourselves and we're much more willing to take risks.

*My Nanna used to say, "If you can put somethin' in your mind's eye and see it, you could do it." I found myself hangin' on to that sayin' when I was in rehab. I just kept seein' myself free of alcohol and drugs and I prayed for my higher power to take the taste outta my mouth, and I truly believed that's what got me through to recovery. My counselor had us keep journals and schedule out our days so that we wouldn't have to guess at what we would be doin' from minute to minute. I still keep a journal but I don't really schedule out my days anymore. Maybe I should start doin' that again.*

*—Cassie*

*I can't really say that I have any new goals or dreams at the present. I mean, my family is in good health, the job thing could be better, but for right now at least I'm workin', and if the good Lord is willin' I'll continue on in that job for a few more years anyway. For a while I was thinkin' about gettin' back in school or just takin' a few classes for fun, but I don't know. I mean, it's not like I really want a whole lot, maybe if I had somethin' to look forward to, I'd be more excited about my life.*

*—Lyndey*

Goals don't have to be monumental projects that require a lot of thought and extended time; we can set small daily goals for ourselves. The idea behind setting goals and writing out an action plan is that it allows us to see what we've accomplished. Often we find ourselves feeling disappointed and depressed because we don't actually believe that we've accomplished anything from one day to the next. This is especially true if the achievement of our goal takes place over a long period of time. For example, I wanted to lose ten pounds, which for me was a long-term goal of at least five months. I knew that if I could do one thing each day it would bring me closer to my long-term goal. So I made the decision to eat one piece of fresh fruit daily. Since I wasn't in the habit of doing so I knew I would need a reminder, so I put it on my daily "to do" list. Each morning when I looked at my list, the first thing I saw staring at me was "eat fresh fruit," so I'd grab an apple and start munching. Every time I finished that piece of fruit and marked it off my list, I could feel better about myself because I knew that I had accomplished one thing that would bring me closer to meeting my overall goal of losing weight.

*Honey, if eatin' that one piece of fruit helped you lose ten pounds, then I think you better sell your story to* The Globe. *I've been tryin' to lose this same twenty pounds for the past fifteen years, and the only thing I've lost is my motivation to ever wear a size ten again.*

—Zoey

It wasn't just eating the one piece of fruit, but actually doing that one thing spurred me on to do other things that were helpful, like making better food choices for myself. This may surprise you, but being motivated isn't the first step in the going for the goal process. The first step is actually taking some form of action. I could have been motivated for five months and never done a thing toward meeting my goal, but taking one step and actually completing it helped me to take the next step and that step led to another step. Each step moved me closer to accomplishing my overall goal. By taking action we move ourselves from a place of ambivalent feelings to a place of feeling hopeful, and when we feel hopeful there's a greater chance that we'll stay on track. We also need to plan rewards for ourselves when we've completed a step toward our goal. Lately I've been rewarding myself with scented candles. At the end of the day I look forward to relaxing in my favorite chair with a good book and enjoying the light and aroma of my candles. It's a simple reward and it gives me a sense of pleasure.

*When I went through the stop smokin' program at the church they really stress the fact that we continue on with the weekly meetin's in order to help us keep our commitment. At first I didn't think I'd keep with it, but now I really look forward to goin' each week, gettin' together with ever'body. I guess you could say that's my reward 'cause I haven' touch a cigarette in four months.*

—Queenie

Congratulations, Queenie, I know you've been wanting to quit for some time now, and it's great that you're continuing on with your meetings. Your weekly meetings are actually serving a dual purpose—you're getting ongoing support for sticking with your goal, and affirming your belief in yourself at the same time. When we have support for ourselves it makes whatever we're doing seem less isolating and difficult.

*I don't generally like to tell other folks when I'm doing somethin' new or different. It's like, what if I mess up or somethin', then I'll never hear the end of it. Besides, I don't like havin' my business out in the street. I remember when my cousin Jolene told everybody she was going to quit her job and move to Atlanta, because she had gotten this great job down there. Well, to make a long story short, the job didn't work out and neither did staying in Atlanta, so she had to move back home. Telling everybody before she had everything set just made her look foolish. Everybody in the family is still talking about her, and it serves her right for telling them.*

*—Ella*

I'm sorry that things didn't work out for your cousin. She took a risk and it didn't pan out but I don't believe that makes her foolish. It's good to have a sense of adventure, and to want to take risks in life, as long as those risks don't endanger yourself or others. Everybody sets goals or makes plans differently. I gave you my formula, which includes laying everything out in steps, but some people aren't comfortable doing things in that manner. They enjoy the challenge of dealing with the unknown and letting the chips fall where they may, which isn't bad, it's just different. However, I agree that it's important to choose our support network carefully. I tend to be selective in whom I choose to confide my plans. Building the courage to take on a new project or a lifestyle change can be difficult so it's valuable to have the encouragement of others who share your vision. Sometimes selecting just one or two others that you feel comfortable enough to share your plan with will be all you need to see you through. Let your support team know what it is that you'd like from them. When I went back to college after a number of years, I chose a couple of friends as my main support

...am. These friends had been through the college re-entry program years before so they knew the ups and downs of getting re-established as a student, and they offered to be my sounding board as I grappled with books, term papers, and finals. I also have a strong group of sister friends that are writers, and we serve as one another's support as we deal with the creative process that often includes deadlines, writer's interruption (we refuse to call it *block*), and the victorious joy of final completion. We offer one another a sense of humor, a sounding board, a shoulder to lean on, hands to hold, and sisterly wisdom (never criticism), and most of all we encourage each other to stay on track.

> *I'm gonna get up in the mornin', wash up a load*
> *of whites, wash down the bathroom, and wax the*
> *livin' and dinin' room floors. Lord, just let me get*
> *through another day.*
>
> —*Momi*

At night as she readied us for bed, Momi would verbally rundown her plans for the following day, always ending with her goal of living through another day. No matter how hard the upcoming tasks were, her plan was often plain and direct (doing the work) and her goal was simple (living through another day). Momi kept a running list of grocery items and doctors' and dental appointments along with each child's school information on a green steno pad with a pencil on the kitchen counter near the phone, and I would see her jot things down in between washing a load of clothes or making a meal. My mother's methods were simple, but they worked as she went about reaching her overall goal . . . living through another day. I often think about my mother's methods of doing things, her ability to accomplish so much with so little, yet she did it, one day at a time.

Someone at one of my readings once asked my mother what she thought of my being a writer, and Momi responded, after singing my praises, "*Well, I always told her she could do anything she wanted to do.*" Actually, Momi did more then tell me, she showed me how to do what I wanted to do. She established a simple plan, enlisted our support, wrote down information, and worked toward her goal. On days when I find myself mentally tripping over my own feet as I struggle to get everything done, I realize that if I take a minute to slow down and listen I can hear Momi whisper in my ear *"Keep it simple, baby, write it down."* If I've learned nothing else from my mother—and I must say I've learned a lot—I learned the value of going for the goal by writing it down and keeping it simple.

## A List of Daily Stress Busters

**Create your own**

Taking a walk
Window shopping
Buying flowers
Going to the gym
Watching
   television
Listening to music
Talking on the
   phone to a friend
Shopping
Daydreaming
Having a nice
   lunch or dinner
Reading a book,
   looking at a
   magazine
Sitting in the sun
Working in
   the garden
Polishing your
   fingernails
Going to a movie
Renting a video
Trying on clothes
   or shoes
Starting a journal
Writing a poem/
   letter
Cooking some-
   thing special

Taking a class
Working a puzzle
Making love
Taking pictures
Watching children
   play
Playing with a pet
Going for a long
   drive
Sewing/knitting
Painting
Taking a class
Getting a
   massage
Taking a nap
Swimming
Singing
Playing solitaire
Jogging
Going to the
   sauna
Yoga
Going to a brown
   bag concert
Taking a bus/cab
   ride

## Getting Things Done

We all have things that we have to get done, and there always seems to be more things to do than there is time to do it. When we become overwhelmed by trying to get everything done two things are sure to happen: We procrastinate, and then we become stressed out, which in turn leads to being depressed because we believe we've failed. There is a way to beat procrastination and stress; it's called planning. Planning helps us to pay attention to the important things in our lives that we want to accomplish short- and long-term. When we prepare a written plan it serves as a blueprint on which we can build our sense of self-worth. Let's face it, we feel good when we accomplish things, even small everyday things. The other bonus of having a written plan is that it relieves the pressure and stress of not having enough time. It's a good idea to remember that written plans aren't carved in stone, they can be adjusted to fit our needs. This exercise will give you two planning options—one for short-term daily projects and one for long-term projects. For the daily plan list three of the most important things that you want to accomplish in the morning, afternoon, and evening. As you complete each task cross it off the list. The goal is not to list everything, but to list the most important things that you want to get done. For example:

**Daily Plan**

| A.M. | Afternoon | P.M. |
|---|---|---|
| 1. Read sales report | 1. Dentist appt. | 1. Dinner with client |
| 2. Sales meeting | 2. Do sales report | 2. Take a hot bath |
| 3. Meet with supervisor | 3. Make two client calls | 3. Read for twenty minutes |

## Long-term Plan

Be as specific as possible when writing your main goal.

Main goal: _____

Steps I need to take: 1. _____

2. _____

3. _____

What do I need in order to complete each step?

Step 1          Step 2          Step 3

_____    _____    _____

_____    _____    _____

_____    _____    _____

How will I reward myself for completing each step of the process?

1. _____

2. _____

Who will be my support through this process?

What distractions might get in the way of my completing these steps?

How will I get back on track?

# The Pleasure Principle

## FAST FACTS
▼▲▼▲▼

Plan one enjoyable activity each day.

Balance work with pleasure.

Enjoyable activities help to relieve stress and tension.

*I love my vacations, it's just that I never get the
chance to take them.*
　　　　　　　　　—Overheard at the beauty shop

When I overheard this snippet of conversation at the beauty shop it struck a chord with me. I'm one of those folks that can plan a vacation down to the very minute details—lying on luscious sun-drenched, sugar-fine sand with crystal blue water lapping at my feet, and a cornflower blue sky overhead, ahhh! . . . now there's my favorite vacation fantasy. However, when it's time for the real deal, I'm so busy rushing around throwing clothes into my suitcase and scrambling to get out of the door that I'm much too exhausted to enjoy the fun I've fantasized about for months. I decided, after spending a hectic two days on my last fantasy vacation wondering if I had turned off the iron, left a nightlight on, and locked the front door, that something had to change. Let's face it, waiting till vacation time rolled around in order to reduce my stress was causing me more stress. When I took an overall view of my last vacation I recognized that I was spending far too much time unwinding and not enough time playing. By the time I got a chance to fully relax and enjoy the precious time that I had fantasized about for months, it was time to start thinking about getting home and back to the grindstone again. I remember asking my mother once what was her favorite vacation, and she said, with a secret smile, *"Every Sunday when your daddy took you all on a long afternoon drive and I stayed home by myself to fix Sunday dinner, now those were my favorite vacations."*

It didn't really make sense at the time, but it does now. My mother learned the art of planned pleasure. As I learned more about depression, one of the things I discovered is that unattended stress robs us of the energy to take pleasure in the things we enjoy most. Putting all of my stress eggs in one basket often left me feeling too fragile to really have fun. If I planned a little something each day to look forward to, it helped me to decrease my stress, and it provided me with the bonus of having enough stamina to make it through to my blowout vacation.

*I'm like your mother. Sundays are my day to kick back, and I let it be known up front. James and the kids can plan anything they want on Sundays but the rule is don't count me in, so he generally packs them off to a movie or a game and I get the whole day and the house to myself.*

—Lyndey

*Well, I think that sounds nice, but Sunday is my church day and that's an all-day affair. I do look forward to my evening television programs, though. Honey, Willie will tell you in a quick second "Don't mess with Queenie when she's watching her nighttime soaps cause she'll hurt you" and he ain't lyin'. I wouldn't mind gettin' away every now and then, but since he retired we don't have the kind of money we used to have, so we just go on little day trips once in a while. But to be real honest my soaps give me all the pleasure I need.*

—Queenie

*I don't know about mini vacations and all that, but since rehab I've learned to use the K.I.S.S. method, which means the Keep It Simple Sweetie method of doin' stuff. When I was using I use to hit the clubs at Happy Hour and kick it till the cows came home. Now that I don't do that anymore, well, it hasn't been easy . . . 'cause all of my old friends are still in the life, so to speak, but I'm into findin' simple ways to have fun. Last week I joined this jazz dance group, and we're goin' be meeting every Thursday and Saturday nights puttin' together little routines.*

—Cassie

It really sounds like you all have the idea. Too often we have the expectation that our pleasurable times should just happen spontaneously, without any thought or planning, or, like me, we're so busying planning in advance and waiting for the good times to roll that we're too wiped out to enjoy them. Being able to balance work with pleasure is a good way of managing our stress levels.

*You all make it sound so easy, but I'm in sales and every minute counts. They've even given us cell phones so that we can take calls from clients when we're away from the office. I can't remember the last time I had a lunch free to myself. But I have to admit that bonus I got sure did look good at the end of the year. I don't mind working; as much as I grumble and complain about my job I really do enjoy having that competitive edge. Besides, I don't know what I'd do on vacation, it's not like I'd have anybody to share it with, and that's most of the fun.*

*—Ella*

*Ella, I can just hear the minister at your funeral sayin' "Here lies Ella Jenkins, she had fun workin' her silly self to death." And the reason you don't have anybody in your life is 'cause you're too dang busy workin' all the time. To be real honest, I was surprised when you said you'd go shoppin' with me. Half the time we don't even see you anymore.*

*—Joyce*

*Joyce is right, Ella, girl, you can't spend that bonus if you're six feet under. You know what they say, the only difference between bein' in a rut and bein' in a grave is the amount of dirt they throw on top.*

*—Zoey*

*I don't think I'm in a rut, Zoey. I know I get stressed out sometimes, but I really do like my job. It's important for me to stay on top. When you lose numbers you lose money, and I've got bills to pay. It's not like anybody's twisting my arm or nothing like that, it's just that my job is a top priority for me right now. Shoot, in another ten years, if I work it right, I'll be able to retire with some money in the bank.*

*—Ella*

*I didn't think I'd be sayin' this, but Ella, honey, some things are more important than workin' twenty-four-seven. You talk about wantin' to be happy, but it doesn't really sound like you've been all that happy lately. It's not like I mean to be dippin' in your business and all, but baby, I just think we're worried about you. I love you like a play sistah, and it just hurts my heart to see you get all run down.*

*—Queenie*

You know I think I can understand where Ella's coming from. It was years before I felt comfortable enough to take a vacation from work, or even plan in a little down time. I worried about job security long before it was a national theme song. I held two jobs for years, with my main priority being to keep food on the table and a roof over my son's head. I believe that I had to be twice or three times better than everybody else, and I thought that the only way I could prove myself was by working long hours. Many of us still don't feel economically safe enough to take time away from our employment.

*I know that's right. Folks are gettin' laid off left and right down at the post office, and I've been pullin' double shifts for two weeks. But I'll tell you this much, I believe in havin' my down time. My kids are old enough to pretty much take care of themselves, so in the evenings when I get off I head straight for the bathroom right after I close the front door, run a hot bath, put on my Marvin Gaye CDs, pour me a lil' taste of Johnny Walker, and put Uncle Sam's mighty mail service far behind me. Between ten and eleven-thirty every night, nobody as much as breathes in my direction, 'cause that is truly my time to unwind. Lord if they ever outlawed those three things I'd be up the creek without a paddle, and you know I can't swim a lick.*

*—Flo*

It sounds like you've got a system in place that lets you cope with your job, Flo, and I don't mean to sound judgmental, but please take care with that little taste of Johnny Walker, because alcohol has been known to add to depression.

*I'm a little like Ella in that I'm not much on big, blowout vacations, although I do enjoy them when I do go on one. But my big thing is music, and ever since the doctor told me I needed to get more exercise I've been taking walks at lunchtime with my Walkman, and I really enjoy it.*

*—Zoey*

*You know, the head teacher at the children's center where I work did something really neat last year for staff Christmas gifts. She gave each of us a gift certificate for a thirty-minute massage. At first I didn't think I'd like it, but you know, it wasn't bad after I got into it. As a matter of fact I've been back a couple of times, and I'm planning to put it in my budget for at least twice a month.*

—*Eboni*

I discovered that if we just plan in twenty minutes of personal stress-free time each day it can make a big difference. It doesn't have to be anything really elaborate, just a little something to lift our spirits and provide a little mental down time. I like to plan in a gym workout at the end of my day. It really gives me something to look forward to after I'm finished with work. On days when I know I can't make it to the gym, I make sure I plan in some other activity to help me relax.

*At my office, we each take turns bringing in coffee break treats on different days of the week. I never really thought about it before, but I find myself really looking forward to going in each morning to see what kind of treat we're going to be having.*

—*Cassie*

*I guess I could work some little things in, but I don't know what that could be. Even if I did take a short vacation I'd still be worried about what's happening at the office. There's a big conference coming up next month in New York, and I was thinking about going. I could tack on a few extra days and do some sight-seeing, but I don't really know anybody there, and I just don't like going places by myself.*

—*Ella*

*Tell you what, sweetcakes, I've got some vacation time comin' and I wouldn't mind seein' some of the East Coast. Maybe we could work it out so that we can go together. But I'm gonna tell you right now, you're gonna have to leave that cell phone at home, 'cause I don't want no unnecessary ringin' to spoil our good time.*

—*Zoey*

*I've been savin' up to go on a cruise this summer, and honey,*
*I can't wait. I've even started workin' weekends at the mini-*
*mart so I'll have extra spending money. Girl, when I hit*
*those ports of call I'm gonna go hog wild, yes indeedy,*
*sweetie, I'm plannin' to have me a ball.*

—*Joyce*

Saving up for a special vacation really sounds like a lot of fun, but don't forget to plan in a little something pleasurable along the way. Working that extra job may add money to our bank accounts but those long hours can take a toll on our stress bank. I'm really in favor of doing a little something special for ourselves on a daily basis. Queenie looks forward to her soaps, Flo has her hot bath; just giving ourselves one special pleasure, something we can count on, makes all the difference in the world. I call my lunchtimes away from the office my stress busters. By taking a little time for myself, I increase my ability to handle other things that come up for me during the day. I think it's important to remember that one of the best ways to decrease depression is by attacking our levels of stress.

## Measure Your Pleasure

As we go about the daily tasks of taking care of family and work responsibilities, it's not uncommon to forget the pleasure of stopping to smell the roses. Many of us forget what it's like to actually relax and enjoy simple pleasures, because we're so caught up in being productive. Research has shown that doing something as simple as taking a five-minute break to stretch can decrease the amount of stress in our lives. Giving ourselves something nice to look forward to each day does two very important things: It increases our emotional stamina and it decreases our stress level. We don't have to plan big, in fact, it's better to plan small. That way we're less likely to rule it out as a pleasurable activity. In fact we may already have little rituals that we do daily without realizing that they give us pleasure. Notice how you feel when you take five or ten minutes to have a cup of coffee or tea, flip through a magazine, or listen to the radio. Rate these activities on a scale of 1 to 5 for pleasure and

plan to do them at least twice a day. If you don't have any little daily rituals now's the time to plan them into your schedule. The following chart will help remind you to take a
pleasure break by having you rate your daily pleasure.

1 ←——————————→ 5

Low                                    High
pleasure                             pleasure

**Monday**        **Pleasurable event**        **Rating**
                  Morning cup of tea           2

                  **Event**                    **Rating**

Monday

Tuesday

Wednesday

Thursday

Friday

Saturday

Sunday

# Show Me a Sign

### FAST FACTS
▼▲▼▲▼

Some things *are* out of our control.

Making a change in a situation can make a change in your mood.

Healing from depression is possible.

> *Girl, you've just described my life.*
>> —Comment from a friend

Marty and I had just finished a leisurely dinner at one of our favorite restaurants, and as we lingered over cups of mint tea, we brought each other up to date on various projects we'd been working on. After giving me a blow-by-blow description of all the backbreaking work she was putting into her new import-export business, Marty settled back with teacup in hand, listening quietly as I described the book I was writing on Black women and depression.

"*I hope you have something in that book that talks about sisters like me,*" she commented quietly as she set her teacup down, staring past me out the window into the darkness of the night sky. "*Girl, you've just described my life.*"

Maybe Marty's admission shouldn't have come as a surprise, but in all honesty, it did. I'd known this woman for fourteen years, and she was the type of sister I'd always aspired to be: beautiful, full of life, and to top it all off, she was an astute businesswoman who always appeared to have her act together. True she could be moody and a tad bit intense at times, but I'd always chalked it up to the fact that she always had a lot on her mind.

"*Don't look so surprised,*" she responded calmly as she reached for the pot of warm tea. "*I've grappled with what you're calling depression for years. I don't talk about it because what's there to say? It's the way I'm wired, so to speak.*"

As Marty talked about her experience, I found myself listening intently, learning about the paradoxical side of depression, in which a person experiences some of the biological symptoms of being depressed, but their symptoms aren't necessarily connected to any type of situational stress. Marty shared with me that while she'd had a number of different stressful situations in her life over the years, she didn't believe that those things had caused her to be depressed.

"*In fact,*" she explained, "*I work better under pressure; I don't consider it stress: I think of it as a challenge, a mental kick in the butt. You know me—I've never been a moaner and complainer; I'm a doer—always have been and always will be. I've never really thought of myself as being depressed. I've got a decent life and most of the time I like who I am, but there's just always been this nagging feeling that I could do a little better. Personally, I just think of it as being my driving force."*

*"Maybe counseling . . ."* I offered, trying not to automatically slip into my therapist mode, but finding it hard not to present a solution.

*"Honey, please! I've been in enough therapy to be able to hang out my own shingle. I've read all the books—self-help, spiritual, new age, you name it, I've read it. After my last divorce, I took Paxil for about six months. It helped me get over the hump, but that's about all, and I started keeping a journal. I still write in it from time to time. Lately, I've just come to the conclusion that I'm not broken—this is the way I am. I guess in the overall grand scheme of things, I've accepted the fact that this is as good as it gets."*

Sitting there listening to Marty and sipping tea, I found my natural curiosity bubbling to the surface. *"How did you know, Marty? What where the signs? How did you come to accept the mood and not fight it?"* I questioned, searching for some sort of clues.

*"Whoa, slow down, girlfriend. I can hear your little mind working. You professionals tickle me—you're always looking for nice neat answers to everything, and I don't know that I have any, to be real honest. Ever since I can remember, I've always been kind of moody. My mother says I'm temperamental; Walt, my ex, used to call me a damn perfectionist, bless his dark soul. I don't know—maybe they're both right. I have some days where I'd call myself temperamental, and there are other days when I'm the perfectionist from hell, but I'd be hard pressed to say I'm either all the time. As for signs, I can't really say that anything in particular stands out for me. I like to have a certain amount of order in my life, if that counts, and like I mentioned before, there's always that little nagging part of me that won't let up. But most of the time I don't really notice it, especially when I'm busy, and you know me—I'm always busy.*

*"If the truth be told, I've never really considered the way I am as a problem. Lately, the only time I've really paid it (that nagging feeling) any attention is when a relationship goes*

*belly-up, and then it's like what's wrong with me, why can't I have and keep a decent relationship? Zoey told me the reason I can't find anybody is because I'm too set in my ways, but you know Zoey: that girl is so laid back it would take a week to roll her up. I just figured that the reason the relationships don't work out is because I refuse to settle for a lot of madness.*

*"I can tell you this much, though,"* she said, reaching for the dinner check, *"I know I'm not alone in feeling the way I do. There are a lot of us sisters running around out there. You professionals call it depression, and I call it my life. Hey, if you decide to put my story in your book, you can call it the invisible face of depression."*

My leisurely dinner with Marty turned out to be a real eye-opener. In writing and talking to sisters I had only focused on the obvious signs and symptoms of depression that sisters need to recognize and address. But as I listened to Marty, I realized that I had completely overlooked what for some of us could be considered almost a personality trait that is in all respects a "normal" part of who we are as individuals. From time to time I had met sisters who, like Marty, appeared to have their lives in perfect order and operated with a level of personal intensity that pushed them into achievement overdrive, but I'd never suspected that they might share many of the symptoms that define depression. Marty described her depression as moodiness, temperament, and perfectionism; however, the usual symptoms and signs of depression—sleeplessness, fatigue, lack of motivation, profound sadness, and indecisiveness, all of which are commonly used as guidelines for assessing depression— were absent from her list.

I thought about Marty's comment, "all of you professionals want nice neat answers." She was partly right, I wryly admitted to myself; the professional therapist in me wanted to explain and find a solution for the problem. And honestly, I didn't see Marty as having the same kind of "problem" that I saw in other depressed sisters. Marty was able to acknowledge her accomplishments and strengths, and make peace with the parts of her life that were less than perfect. I wondered, though, if it was the absence of the typical symptoms and signs that allowed Marty to view her depression as being "invisible." Although she chose to see the visible symptoms of depression as being more of "a mental kick in the butt," she still seemed to have a suspicion that even with all she'd accomplished, an intangible "more" was possible for her. I wondered, in fact, where that might lead if she took it further.

As a professional I'm trained to look for signs and symptoms, visible evidence that points to a problem. And most of the sisters I'd worked with saw their depression as a direct result of what they were dealing with at the time. But what if there was a recurring mood without the other obvious symptoms—did that still mean there was a problem?

I was raised to believe that signs always precede significant events of some sort. Mama, my grandmother, was a great believer in the practice of observing signs. If her right palm itched, it was a sign that she was going to get some money; if she dreamt about fish, it was a sure sign that a woman in the family was pregnant. I would consider that "nagging feeling" Marty's sign, the thing that just might challenge her to take some kind of action. Perhaps our dinner conversation was her way of starting.

Not long after I had dinner with Marty I attended a professional conference, where during the question and answer period one of the participants brought up the theory that people who experience ongoing episodes of depression are actually addicted to being in control of their environments and their lives. The conference speaker gave a response with which I strongly agree (I'm paraphrasing): There are some people who have somewhat depressive natures, and while they might experience episodes of clinical depression from time to time, these individuals are much more likely to be committed to a measure of structure and responsibility, and their clinical signs of depression are most often a sign that their sense of structure has been severely disrupted. This response certainly fit in Marty's case, in the relationship area, and it also fit for another sister that I had worked with, who had been experiencing difficulties in her work environment.

I don't believe that desiring a level of control is necessarily "bad." We all aspire to have control over certain portions of our lives; it allows us to experience certain amounts of individual freedom. But let's face it—given the ethnic and cultural climate alone, there are things outside our control: Racism is real for Black women, and we are going to find ourselves in situations, especially on the job, where we don't have control over another individual's prejudices. Sexism is real, too: sisters who have dealt with sexual harassment on the job will attest to that. Even when we want to ignore it, it doesn't always ignore us. It doesn't have to dictate the level at which we choose to function in our lives, however. Being in or out of control doesn't automatically account for being depressed, although for in-control sisters, it's a good sign to be aware of—a sign that when our sense of balance or control is compromised, we may experience emotional fallout.

Does doing something different—leaving a relationship, for example, or starting a new one, moving or changing jobs—to address a "nagging feeling" like Marty's mean that depression will go away? My answer is both yes and no, and that is what I call the paradox of depression. Addressing the depression first, as depression, on the basis of how severe the symptoms are, and beginning to feel a lessening of the symptoms, will allow you to determine what changes really need to be made to improve the overall quality of your life. On the other hand, relief from an immediate situation—like leaving a toxic work situation for something you'd prefer to do, even if you have to take a cut in pay—might solve the problem, at least temporarily. If the symptoms return even when the problem has been solved, it's important to remember that there are still a number of options for dealing with depression.

In one of my workshops recently, one of the women asked if it was ever possible to heal from depression. Without a doubt the answer is yes, healing is always possible, but the first step in healing is knowing what you're dealing with, which is why understanding the signs of depression is so very important. Depression, in and of itself, while emotionally painful, is not a death sentence—it's the severity of the symptoms that cause us difficulty and that require medical attention. Depression is not a sign that we're broken; it's a sign that tells us that we might want to take steps to structure a healing process in our lives.

# Gradual Awakening

## FAST FACTS
▼▲▼▲▼

Healing begins by taking one step.

Doing one thing differently each day can make a difference.

TURNING

*turning into my own*
*turning on in*
*to my own self*
*at last*
*turning out of the*
*white cage, turning out of the*
*lady cage*
*turning at last*
*on a stem like a black fruit*
*in my own season*
*at last*

—Lucille Clifton
*Good Woman: poems and a memoir 1969–1980*

I don't remember the exact time or date, but I do remember feeling good. Not happy, not excited, just plain old good down to the bone, that warm comfortable sensation that wraps you in the security blanket of being in your own skin, that luscious kind of good where you hug yourself and thank God for being alive. Toweling off after a steamy hot shower, I heard myself humming along to Anita Baker's latest hit as I smoothed cocoa butter lotion on my arms and legs. While calmly going about my daily routine of getting ready for work, it suddenly dawned on me that it had been a long time since I felt good enough to hum along to a song. For that matter, it had been rare in the past few weeks that I even took the time to notice what was on the radio, let alone listen closely enough to hum along. The more I thought about it the more I recognized that what was truly different was the fact that I felt alive, as in not depressed. For the first time in weeks I wasn't struggling with the cloudy haze of thoughts that had kept my mind bound in an endless web of doubt and confusion. I truly felt as if I had been "Caught Up in the Rapture" of being alive.

"*What was different for you?*" my therapist asked, as I lounged on the overstuffed soft white leather couch, absorbing the unusually bright sun beaming through the stained glass picture window in her cozy office.

*"I don't know. I just feel good. I don't want to analyze it, I just want to feel and enjoy it,"* I responded smugly.

*"I agree, I think you should enjoy feeling good."* She nodded while handing me a cup of fragrant orange spice tea. *"And while I agree that we don't have to analyze it, I think it might be a good idea to talk about the process of how you came to this place of well-being. After all, I'm aware that you've felt good in the past, and I'm also aware that just as your good feelings come and go, so does your depression."*

*"Maybe it was magic,"* I replied playfully, with some concern that getting serious would erase my sense of calm.

*"I don't think so, but if that's true, then that means you're the magician, and all good magicians have a tried-and-true technique for pulling the rabbit out of the hat. So let's talk, shall we?"* she countered with a sly smile.

My therapist was right, my sense of feeling good wasn't magic; it wouldn't vanish into a cloud of smoke if I dared to touch the core of my wellness. My pleasant mood was part of a larger process of which my depression had played a major role. I believed that talking about the healing would mean exposing the depth of the darkness, conjuring up the hurt and pain that had taken me weeks to overcome, but— and I'm not ashamed to admit it—I was wrong. My gradual awakening had—as many things in life generally do—a beginning. My healing began the day I called my depression by name and accepted the honest fact that depression would always be a strong thread woven tightly into the fabric of my life.

I remember mentioning to a friend at one point that I thought I was depressed.

*"Girl, please! That's truly a luxury we Black folk just can't afford. Come on now, I know things are a little tough right now, but you're strong enough to handle it."*

My friend's comment wasn't made with malice, she was speaking a stereotypical truth that has plagued us as Black women for centuries. We're "strong enough to handle it," the "it" being wounds of passion, traumatic hurts, economic struggles, and family hardships that would somehow be instantly absorbed by our supposed strength. I remember thinking, "How can I tell her that I no longer want to embrace the struggle of being a strong Black woman, or explain that my illusion of strength had become a steel vise that was squeezing the life out of my body?" My fear of her disapproval made me laugh quietly, while offering a meager "Yeah, you're right" acknowledgment, knowing inwardly that I would have to seek my solution for support elsewhere.

I started taking anti-depressant medication in the fall of 1995. It was a slow, gradual awakening after a hellish, restless, eight-month sleep. After careful consideration I agreed to a trial of anti-depressant medication for six months to a year, coupled with solution-focused therapy in order to build appropriate problem-solving skills. I wish I could say that I started taking the medication one night, went to sleep, and rolled out of bed the next day healed, although I've heard testimonies of miracle healing of this sort from various others who had made the decision to take anti-depressants. My healing was a slow, steady, and sometimes painful process in which I learned how to sort out the reality of my present situation from the confusing haze of the depression. Over a period of several weeks as I continued to take the medication, I experienced a progressive sense of lightness, as in not feeling burdened or weighted down by the thought of making it through another day. I began to notice and take pleasure in small things: humming to a song on the radio, the slippery coolness of cocoa butter lotion on my skin, and the ease of not feeling rushed. Several weeks after I started using medication I happened to be browsing through some old magazines in the library and I came across the story of Phyllis Hyman's suicide. I stood transfixed in the middle of the aisle reading the story, complete with pictures of her home, of how Phyllis Hyman, a talented Black songstress who had won numerous awards and honors for her work on the stage as well as in the movies, had taken her own life at the peak of her career. The article spoke of how various friends and family members had known that Ms. Hyman suffered from issues of self-doubt and struggled with her weight, and they had even encouraged her to seek help from time to time, but no one thought it would end like this . . . in death. After reading the article twice, I went away from the library that day convinced that Phyllis Hyman didn't only suffer from depression, she also suffered from the ravages of being that "strong Black woman, who could handle it." As I drove home, listening to the gentle sweet melody of Sweet Honey in the Rock, I found myself reflecting on all the reasons that I had chosen to get help: I was scared, I was tired of pretending that I wasn't scared, and I needed supportive help, a form of help that would allow me to cope without the additional burden of guilt that I recognized as helplessness. As I thought about these reasons, I wondered if any of them meant that I wasn't strong in the ethnic sense, and I decided that the answer was no. I also wondered if Phyllis Hyman or any of the other sisters (and there have been a number of them) who had taken the final step of suicide had wrestled with the same types of issues, and again the answer was clear, of course they had—the overwhelming pain of depression coupled with the resounding belief that one has failed at being "strong enough to handle it" could lead one to take drastic measures. Sitting at the stop light waiting for it to change, I felt my eyes fill with tears, tears for Phyllis, and all the other sisters who had died suffering in silence from the pain of being strong. I also shed tears for myself, tears of release, because I knew that I didn't have to suffer in silence any longer. I could give up being strong enough to handle it, and embrace being strong enough to be human.

Will the depression come back? I wish I could paint a lovely picture and say "no," that I've climbed that mountain and this phase of my life is behind me, never to be revisited. However, that's not the case. Statistical data drawn from the National Institute of Mental Health states that in all likelihood individuals will experience several episodes of major depression during their lifetime. My mother's death was not my first episode of depression; however, it was by far my worst, and I have every reason to believe that it won't be my last. As Sweet Honey and the Rock sings, *"Nobody knows what tomorrow will bring."* When asked if I would be willing to use anti-depressant medication again, the answer I give without hesitation is always "yes." This experience was a great teacher for me in many ways. The lesson that stands out the most is that human suffering is not a requirement for life, nor is the pain of being strong worthy of my life. Phyllis Hyman may have sung the blues, but I believe that she was crying out for help. In a statement released after her death, her family called her suicide "a wake-up call for everyone in pain" and they encouraged others to seek help. As Black women many of us have been in pain much too long, and Phyllis's family recognizes, as do I, that we don't have to stay in that place, we can move to a place of peace by seeking help.

Using anti-depressant medication was a difficult decision for me to make. I made the decision and I'm not sorry for it, or for the fact that the medication and therapy saved the quality of my emotional life. I've come to recognize that the medication didn't make me "feel good," it restored the emotional energy that I needed to reclaim that part of myself that's always been available to me but was inaccessible largely due to the depression. I discovered that when I laid down the burden of depression, I could pick up the comfort of peace.

# Further Information: Dealing with the Healing

### FAST FACTS
▼▲▼▲▼

Healing from depression is an up and down process.

Healing from depression happens in stages.

It's important to have an accurate diagnosis.

You have already taken your first step toward healing.

One of the most difficult parts of my experience with depression was not in the process of healing; it was in the acknowledgment that something other than "human weakness" was the problem. The idea that I could actually heal came as a blessed relief after weeks and months of internal struggle with my fears. I went for months knowing that something wasn't right, but I was afraid to find out what it was, and in this vein I'm sure that I'm not alone. Not dealing with the depression gave me the false sense that my life was out of my control. It was only after being able to name my discontent that I could actually take some comfort in knowing I still had control of my life. The information in this section offers a few more ways to help you recognize the signs of depression.*

## Symptoms of Depression

The National Institute of Health has developed the following checklist:

Persistent sad or "empty" mood
Loss of interest or pleasure in ordinary activities, including sex
Decreased energy, fatigue, being "slowed down"
Sleep disturbances: insomnia, early-morning waking, or oversleeping
Eating disturbances: loss of appetite and weight, or weight gain
Difficulty concentrating, remembering, making decisions
Feelings of guilt, worthlessness, helplessness
Thoughts of death or suicide, suicide attempts
Irritability
Excessive crying
Chronic aches and pains that don't respond to treatment

If four or more of these symptoms have been a regular part of your life for more than two weeks, please consult with your physician.

*From "How to Heal Depression," Harold H. Bloomfield, M.D., & Peter McWilliams.

## Most-Asked Questions

**What is depression?** Depression is a complex emotional disorder with diverse symptoms, a variety of causes, and a wide range of effects on each individual it touches. There are three main types of depression:

Major Depression: usually associated with a traumatic event of some kind such as death, divorce, breakup of a relationship, relocating, or a job loss or change. The symptoms usually have a recognizable beginning, middle, and ending point. The lingering feelings of emotional hurt and profound sadness can last anywhere from a couple of weeks to months.

Chronic Depression: a low-grade, long-term depression that can go on for years. Many people have had chronic depression for most of their lives, starting in childhood. It's believed that this type of depression may be associated with childhood trauma.

Manic-depression: this type of depression alternates the low mood with a manic or high mood, which consists of extreme elation, inappropriate behaviors, grandiose thoughts, and sometimes destructive behavior.

**How do I know that I'm really depressed?** Depression can be broken down into four general symptoms: how you *feel*: guilty, sad, helpless; how you *act*: slowed down, fatigued, low energy; how you *think*: negative view of yourself, the world, and the future; and how your *body re-acts*: trouble sleeping, unexplained aches and pains, changes in your eating patterns. If three or more of these symptoms are present for two weeks or more there's a good chance that you're experiencing some form of depression.

**What causes depression?** It's really difficult to establish a simple cause-and-effect relationship in regard to depression. Even when we know the exact trigger of an episode of depression, such as the death of a loved one or a job loss, it's often difficult to evaluate if that's the only cause. However, we do know that most cases of major depression (which is the most common type) appear to be triggered by unresolved stresses.

**What's the difference between depression and just having a case of the blues?** The symptoms for major depression and the characteristics of the blues look very similar, in that they share a recognizable beginning, middle, and end in terms of the sadness or low period. One of the main differences, however, is that generally the blues doesn't last longer than two weeks.

**Is there a cure for depression?** Within the mental health profession we recognize that life stresses tend to be too unpredictable to offer a blanket "yes" or "no" in terms of a cure for depression. We know that some people experience fewer episodes of depression for shorter periods of time, while other people seem to get depressed more often and for longer periods. While it's difficult to understand exactly what causes the difference, we do know that those who experience less depression tend to have better life-coping skills. For that reason it's much wiser to look at depression in terms of recovery, the goal being that with treatment a person would experience fewer episodes of depression, with each episode lasting for a shorter period of time.

**Do I have to take medication?** Again, this is not a simple "yes" or "no" answer. It's been established that if the depression is recognized in the very early stages, treatment without medication is possible. However, in some situations, which are dependent on the length of time and the intensity of the symptoms, the use of medication for depression would be considered a realistic option. Generally medication is considered when any of the following conditions are present: (1) a person's depression is severe; (2) there have been at least two prior depressive episodes; (3) there is a family history of depression; and (4) the person specifically requests the use of medication.

**I heard that a lot of people use a natural herb called St. John's wort for their depression. What is it?** St. John's wort or *Hypericum perforatum*, as it's officially known, is a perennial herb. It's been widely and very effectively used in Germany and the rest of Europe for years in the treatment of mild to moderate depression. Currently St. John's wort can't be prescribed medically due to U.S. Food and Drug

Administration regulations. After doing very thorough and extensive research studies on its effectiveness, however, many health care professionals are recommending its use for mild to moderate depression, in dosages of .3% Hypericum; 300mg, three times daily.

**Will I become addicted to the medication?** No. There are several types of antidepressants which include tricyclic antidepressants (TCAs), monoamine oxidase inhibitors (MAOIs), and selective serotonin reuptake inhibitors (SSRIs); however, none of these medications are habit-forming in any way.

**What if I don't want to use medication?** Treatment would still be available, in the form of psychotherapy.

**Will treatment be covered by my insurance?** Most but not all medical insurance plans cover mental health treatment. Individual plans differ, however, in specific areas: For example, medications used in treatment may not be covered, or you may be limited in the number of visits or the type (educational background) of therapist you can work with in treatment. It's always best to check with your provider in order to be on the safe side.

**How long will I have to be in treatment?** Psychotherapy treatment for depression does not have to be a long process. In fact, recent research and study by the National Institute of Mental Health shows that the most effective therapy is brief (eight to twelve weeks), solution-focused (works to solve the current problem), and builds skills for coping. Cognitive, behavioral, and interpersonal psychotherapy are three of the effective approaches for therapy that follow these guidelines.

**Will I have to talk about my problems in front of a bunch of other people?** No. However, group treatment is an option that is often recommended for a couple of reasons: (1) Group treatment cuts down on the isolation that people often experience with depression. Unlike process-treatment groups in which people examine their personal issues by just talking, skill-building groups are designed like classes in which people work through their depression by doing various assignments and reporting their results in the group. The other factor is that often insurance companies will lower rates for individuals involved in group programs, which can make treatment more affordable.

**What if I don't want to go and talk to anybody, can I get better on my own?** Some people have been known to recover from depression on their own without seeing a therapist by using any number of self-help aids, i.e., books, workbooks, and audio tapes. However if the symptoms are persistent, or there are suicidal feelings present, it's strongly recommended that you contact a professional at once.

**Will other people know that I'm depressed?** If the symptoms are intense enough that they cause changes in your behavior or mood there's a good chance that people will know that something is not right, but they wouldn't necessarily know what's wrong with you.

**Would I have to tell my supervisor or other people on my job?** No. Who you choose to tell will always be your choice. If your work is being affected by the depression, for example—if you're not getting to work on time, not finishing assignments, or you need to take time off—it may be a good idea to let your supervisor know what's going on, but again it's your choice.

**How do I know I can trust the person I'm working with?** Trust is an important issue in treatment, and it does take time to develop a trusting relationship. If you're comfortable letting your friends know that you're seeking a therapist, ask them for recommendations or ask your doctor for a referral to a mental health specialist. Once you've met the therapist, ask her or him questions that will help you to get to know them as a professional. Questions regarding their educational background, years of practice, and expertise in working with depression are all appropriate. Consider your comfort and ease in being able to develop rapport. I generally suggest meeting with someone at least twice in order to get a read on comfort level; however, some people have known after one session if they made a good connection.

**Would I be better off talking to a therapist of color?** That's really a matter of personal preference. Some of us feel more comfortable talking to a professional sister or brother, in the belief that they will be more in touch with "our reality"–based situations. However, the main criteria should always be comfort and the therapist's level of expertise.

# Additional Reading

*On the Edge of Darkness: Conversations About Conquering Depression* by Kathy Cronkite, Doubleday, 1994.

*Willow Weep for Me: A Black Woman's Journey Through Depression* by Meri Nana-Ama Danquah, W.W. Norton, 1998.

*Feeling Good: The New Mood Therapy* by David Burns, M.D., William Morrow, 1989.

*Beat Depression with St. John's Wort* by Steven Bratman, M.D., Prima, 1997.

*An Unquiet Mind* by Kay Redfield Jamison, Ph.D., Simon & Schuster, 1995.

*Darkness Visible: A Memoir of Madness* by William Styron, Vintage, 1992.

*Breaking the Patterns of Depression* by Michael D. Yapko, Ph.D., Doubleday, 1997.

*How to Heal Depression* by Harold H. Bloomfield, M.D., and Peter McWilliams, Prelude, 1996.

# Workshops and Lectures

For a listing of Julia A. Boyd's workshops and lectures, or if you're interested in having one in your area, please write to her at the address below. She welcomes feedback to *Can I Get a Witness?* but regrets that she is unable to answer individual letters.

Julia A. Boyd
31849 Pacific Highway South #155
Federal Way, Washington 98003

Or visit her website:

http://www.jetcity.com/~gumbomed/jbhome.htm